Praise for *Outrageous Fortunes*

"If the past two years have taught us anything, it is the importance of counterintuitive thinking. Daniel Altman boldly ventures into the deep drivers of global change to uncover the unintended consequences of our current policies—regarding China, global trade, American jobs, and much more. Anyone who wants to get smart on globalization's fate must read this book."

—Parag Khanna, author of *The Second World* and *How to Run the World*

"With so many new books offering autopsies of the financial crisis and the deepest recession since World War II, it's a blessing that Daniel Altman has his eyes firmly fixed on risks and opportunities in the road ahead. He brings together a series of compelling predictions, and though readers may not agree with every element of his forecasts, all will be better informed for having read his book."

—Ian Bremmer, president of Eurasia Group and author of *The End of the Free Market* and *The J Curve*

"With all the attention being lavished on the short-run gyrations of the economy, it is refreshing to see a book that focuses on the long run. Daniel Altman is brave enough to make predictions about what will happen to the world economy twenty or thirty years from now. His analysis is thoughtful and compelling and should be required reading for those interested in creating a better world for our offspring."

—Hal R. Varian, chief economist at Google and professor of business, economics, and information management at the University of California, Berkeley

"Amid all the handwringing on the downward trajectory of the global economy comes this cool, collected, and sensible view of forthcoming economic trends. . . . Altman delivers more than mere analysis or foreshadowing: This is revelatory reading for even the most casual observer of economics, and an invaluable tool for reconsidering how the world makes money."

—*Publishers Weekly* (starred review)

OUTRAGEOUS FORTUNES

THE TWELVE SURPRISING TRENDS THAT WILL RESHAPE THE GLOBAL ECONOMY

DANIEL ALTMAN

ST. MARTIN'S GRIFFIN
NEW YORK

Designed by Kelly S. Too

www.stmartins.com

The Library of Congress has cataloged the Henry Holt edition as follows:

Altman, Daniel, 1974–
    Outrageous fortunes : the twelve surprising trends that will reshape the global economy / Daniel Altman.—1st ed.
        p. cm.
    Includes bibliographical references and index.
    ISBN 978-0-8050-9102-1
    1. Economic forecasting.   I. Title.
    HB3730.A625 2011
    330.9—dc22

                                                        2010018877

ISBN 978-1-250-00173-3 (trade paperback)

Originally published in hardcover format by Times Books, an imprint of Henry Holt and Company

First St. Martin's Griffin Edition: January 2012

10 9 8 7 6 5 4 3 2 1

To Hari Seldon

CONTENTS

PREFACE TO THE
PAPERBACK EDITION

I finished writing the first edition of this book in November 2009. By the time it arrived on store shelves, virtual, and otherwise, I had a creeping suspicion that some of my predictions were already coming true. With time, the feeling has only intensified. I must admit that this has been something of a surprise, given that my forecasting horizon was decades—not months or years—into the future.

Yet whenever I looked around the global economy and read what people were saying about it, the evidence seemed to be piling up. First, the euro came under threat as Greece begged for bailout upon bailout to avoid defaulting on its debt. As Spain and Italy struggled to avoid being next in line, it was fast becoming obvious that a single monetary policy would not suit all of Europe. Indeed, within a month of this book's publication, a headline in the *Financial Times* blared, "All aboard for a new two-speed Europe." Soon there would have to be a process for exiting the euro zone, not just one for entering.

The writing was on the wall in other areas, too. Susan Schwab, the former United States Trade Representative who had spent most of her time in office trying to save the World Trade Organization's Doha Development Round of global negotiations, called in *Foreign Affairs* for the very same talks to be abandoned. A couple of months later, the United States finally joined the race to lure the highest-skilled immigrants from the developing world by moving toward what Vivek Wadhwa, a columnist for *The Washington Post*, called a "start-up visa": an easier path to permanent residency for entrepreneurs whose companies served the nation's economic interests.

In the meantime, the short-term thinking among politicians in Washington, with their two-year electoral cycle less than halfway over, almost left the Treasury unable to pay its debts—a shocking turn of events for what was supposedly the world's most reliable borrower. Even though the dreaded default was averted, the manufactured minicrisis still caused widespread uncertainty, sent risk managers scurrying to rebalance their portfolios, and triggered staggering drops in stock markets around the world. These political leaders, with their never-ending campaigns and decisions motivated more by political opportunism than economic wisdom, weren't up to the task of solving the nation's long-term fiscal woes.

TO me, a clear message from the world's recent economic tribulations has been the importance of long-term thinking, which also happens to provide the foundation for this book. Even in the throes of an economic downturn that presents a new danger almost every week, farsighted governments, companies, and individuals have fared better than those focused on the short term.

Latvia, for example, was caught in a severe crunch during the global financial crisis. Unlike Greece, however, it decided to swallow the bitter pill as soon as possible, raising interest rates and making massive cuts to government budgets while ensuring that its social safety net would continue to catch the hardest-hit victims on their way down. The idea was to pay a high up-front cost in order to regain the confidence of lenders and bolster growth for the future. Within a year, Latvia was well on its way to economic recovery and had restored its credibility in international markets, while Greece still limped along with the half-measures that emerged from parliamentary bickering.

Similarly, Jamie Dimon, the chief executive of JPMorgan Chase, became the toast of the financial world for steering his big bank through the crisis better than any of his counterparts. Analysts pointed to his long-term thinking—stopping risky lending practices, putting in place a long-term succession plan, and tying portfolio managers' pay to clients' long-term returns—as the reasons for his success. Even while the crisis was raging, JPMorgan Chase found time to take the lead in long-term thinking about so-called "social" or "impact" investments, using them as a way to cultivate a new customer base while burnishing the bank's reputation.

Long-term thinking also leads to better economic forecasting. My intent in this book is to show how combining logic with an understanding of the deep factors that cause economic shifts can lead to counterintuitive yet often inescapable predictions for the long term. To put it another way, forecasting is like seismology; you have to look deep below the surface, identify the continental plates that are shifting, measure their directions, gauge their momentum, and then calculate how they'll interact over the course of many years. If you just counted the number of earthquakes observed above ground, how could you have any idea what the future would hold?

I find applications for this approach all the time. Shortly before this book was first published, I was asked to give a lecture about political economy in South America. For decades, countries there had swung like pendulums between left-wing populism and right-wing authoritarianism. Why had some of them finally settled down into stable patterns of economic growth? As living standards rose, I suggested, people had something to lose; they began to prefer centrist governments and would no longer follow a radical demagogue wherever he might lead them. Typically, the countries that managed to still their pendulums had gone through two final swings. First, they elected center-right governments that installed probusiness policies that attracted foreign investment. Then, they elected center-left governments that kept these policies in place but legitimized them through redistribution, so that everyone could share in the benefits of growth. So it went in Brazil, Chile, and Uruguay, and I suggested in a lecture in January 2011 that Peru could follow suit if the center-left leader Ollanta Humala were elected president. He was, and *The Economist* soon asked, "The Brazilian way: But will it work in Peru?"

The combination of logic and deep factors can be useful for some short-term predictions, too. Take the revolutions of the Arab Spring—why did some end quickly and with little bloodshed, while others are still taking lives every day? Looking beneath the surface can offer an answer. For instance, before its revolution, Tunisia already had a better business climate than some countries in the European Union. The Tunisian people had something worth protecting, but they still lacked opportunity. Naturally, they wanted to move closer to meritocracy without destroying the foundations of their country's growth, and the revolution was brief and relatively painless. In Libya, however, the working class has little to lose, while the country's tiny elite has everything. These are the ingredients of a fight to the death.

DURING one of the darkest moments of the global financial crisis, a contact called me up and said breathlessly that it must have been a fantastic time to be writing about economics. I replied that I took no joy in the tribulations that were costing millions of people their livelihoods and their savings. I feel the same way about seeing my predictions come true; many of them were meant to be cautionary tales about what might come to pass, were we to ignore the most pressing problems in our midst. A gloomy prediction, indeed, should be seen as an opportunity to adjust, to improve, and to choose a different fate. As Charles Dickens wrote, in the person of Ebenezer Scrooge in *A Christmas Carol*:

> Men's courses will foreshadow certain ends, to which, if persevered in, they must lead. But if the courses be departed from, the ends will change.

I am sure he intended this axiom to apply to women, too. Outdated conventions aside, it is still my hope that this book will have a positive and empowering effect on our world. By looking far into the future, we give ourselves enough time to change it. Let us not miss the opportunity.

Daniel Altman
September 2011

INTRODUCTION

The global economy is changing more quickly than ever before in its history. The technologies that have made it more integrated—primarily those that have improved transportation and the exchange of information—continue to develop, and the number of interactions among people from all parts of the world is growing exponentially. These changes are having a profound effect on our lives. In the past two decades, we have seen hundreds of millions of people escape poverty, but we have also seen a severe deterioration in our natural environment and the bursting of huge financial bubbles.

Despite the refinement of economic policies designed to manage the business cycle, the volatility of commodity prices, trade flows, government budgets, and many other important indicators of the global economy continues to increase. As a result, it is easy to get caught up in the stream of numbers that spew out every second and to lose sight of the long term. That's a problem for our future. Personal fortunes may be gained and lost in a day, but national fortunes are gained and lost because of deeply ingrained economic factors that take years to develop and, if necessary, to change. Certainly, idiosyncratic events can push countries to one side or the other of their long-term economic paths. But over the course of decades, those paths tend to be determined by economic factors with very deep roots indeed.

These deep factors do not necessarily explain why stock markets rise and fall in the course of a single day, hour, or minute, but they do set limits on the material standards of living that an economy can achieve. If the pursuit of economic growth is a race, then these factors determine the location of the finish line. Because the finish line can often seem very far away, however, they do not receive very much attention in the daily pronouncements of pundits, politicians, and even people who know a little bit of economics.

This book aims to change that. It begins by explaining how, over long periods of time, countries with similar deep factors tend to reach similar limits of growth and prosperity. Those limits will start to bind, perhaps sooner rather than later, for the current darling of the global economy, China. China's rapid growth—and the notion that this growth will continue for decades to come—has attracted investment from around the world. Yet its long-term prospects are not as rosy as investors might hope. The European Union has also been a popular target for investors because of its political stability, its huge internal market, and the potential of its newer Eastern members. Its euro currency has given central banks, sovereign wealth funds, and other major investors a long-awaited alternative to the dollar. But all is not well in the Union, nor in the euro area, both of which are beginning to fall apart because the member countries are facing different limits to growth.

As countries strive to reach their limits and offer their citizens the highest possible living standards, they will come upon a series of obstacles. Their economies need resources—both natural and human—as well as a certain measure of stability. In the coming decades, many countries will face shortages of all three of these items, and those shortages will slow their headlong dash toward the finish line. Some countries will colonize others in a bid to secure the natural resources their economies need to grow: raw materials for manufacturing, crops to feed workers, fuel, and water. This time, the colonial conquests will be achieved through monetary rather than military means, but the results will likely be counterproductive for both the colonizers and the colonized. Rich countries, with their aging populations and low fertility rates, will change their immigration policies to draw in more workers from around the world. Even as poor countries develop, it will be harder for them to hold on to their most productive citizens. Meanwhile, many countries that have embraced left-leaning populist governments in recent years will first shift to the right, then continue to swing back and forth like political pendulums. The resulting regime changes will slow their economic growth—an unfortunate reality, since growing may be the only way to settle the pendulums down.

In the midst of these limits and obstacles, there will also be new opportunities. As the booms fueled by technology and cheap credit in the 1990s and 2000s fade into the background, Americans will be looking for new sources of jobs and income. They will find some of them in an unexpected place, drawing on a little-recognized but fundamental pillar of their nation's economic success: selling power. The restructuring of the global economy—ever more intertwined, ever more digital—will also allow workers to seize new opportunities by straddling two or more markets at a time and acting as gatekeepers of profit. Changes in how people work will lead them to change where they work as well; in the future, a growing class of mobile professionals will populate a new set of economic hubs founded on lifestyle choices rather than business imperatives. And the slow collapse of the World Trade Organization will actually allow countries to pursue freer trade, opening up new gains from doing business abroad.

Despite the opportunities it presents, the road to growth is not always smooth. Even if a country manages to avoid the obstacles along its particular path, there are still risks that affect everyone in the race. The recent financial crisis showed that negligence, malfeasance, and herd behavior in a couple of financial centers can stunt growth around the world, setting some countries back years in their pursuit of higher living standards. One result of the new regulatory framework facing the world of finance will be the blossoming of an enormous black market whose presence will bring new risks to the global economy. At the same time, climate change—often touted as an opportunity for new industries in rich and poor countries alike—will actually separate these countries even further, creating a threat of instability that could hamper growth in both. To solve these problems, countries will have to work together. Yet the political institutions that provide the framework for global problem-solving may not be up to the task.

EVEN generalists have their areas of strength and weakness, so this book does not take on every pressing economic issue. Other writers are better equipped to predict which fuel will power the transport of the future (indeed, some already have), which super- and semi-conductors will carry the global economy's data, and whether that mode of transport and those data will help humankind to develop the resources of the moon, other planets, or faraway galaxies. The task of prediction is difficult enough without venturing so far afield in so many different directions.

Only recently, in fact, have economists truly begun to understand just how difficult prediction is, both at the individual level and for an entire economy. Through the 1960s, as the science of economics lurched toward maturity, an implicit part of many economists' predictions was the notion that people would make the same mistakes time and again. For example, if consumers saw a big increase in their salaries, they might take it as a signal of bigger buying power, even if the raise was always followed by an increase in prices for the things they liked to buy. In the 1970s, a new school of economics began to hold sway. It was based on the opposing idea that people were too rational to make the same mistake twice; consumers might be fooled by the raise the first time, but the second time they'd wait to see if inflation would erase their apparent gains. This new school dominated economic thought for a couple of decades, before another revolution in economic thinking came along in the waning years of the twentieth century: behavioral economics. The behavioralists, sitting at the intersection of economics and psychology, saw that people might seem rational at a moment in time but were not always consistent over the long term. They asked why people deliberately did things that they regretted in retrospect, and why people could not always commit themselves to act in a certain way in the future. No behavioralist would be surprised if people who understood inflation perfectly well went out to spend part of their raise. Unlike the economists of the 1960s, though, the behavioralists didn't think these people were being fooled by their raises. Instead, they probably thought these people could not resist the temptation to spend, perhaps figuring that they would scrimp in the future to make up for it—but only if they had to.

For several decades, economists have realized that simply extrapolating trends is not the best way to predict the future (though this does not stop many from continuing to do it). The move toward behavioral economics has helped to make sense of some economic trends, especially those that change suddenly as mob psychology or hysteria takes over. Nonetheless, economics still isn't very good at forecasting those sudden changes, either in their direction or their timing.

This is partly because economists still don't completely understand how people's minds work, but it's also because they often focus on the wrong things. A huge chunk of the world's economic brainpower is focused on the financial markets, where the typical time horizon ranges from a few minutes to three months. Whether it's a snap trade to offset risk in a derivatives market, or a prediction of a company's quarterly earnings, there's not much thinking about the long term. Even the more academic economists who work at places like the World Bank and the Organization for Economic Cooperation and Development usually think about the long term as a period of just five or ten years. For this reason, they often neglect the deep factors that really move the global economy over the course of decades.

Yet those deep factors are the most important ones. They will determine whether entire generations—hundreds of millions of people—live better or worse than their predecessors. The deep factors' origins lie in geography, climate, culture, politics, and historical accident. They are so powerful that they can swamp the effects of thousands of discrete events that may seem hugely important when they occur, such as the bankruptcy of General Motors or the re-election of Hugo Chávez as Venezuela's president.

Some economists, to whom I will refer later in the book, have begun to study these deep factors, for instance, by tracing how the systems of government set up by colonial powers in the eighteenth and nineteenth centuries have affected the scope of financial markets in the twenty-first. But by and large, these important forces are still neglected and poorly understood.

The first task of this book is to rectify that situation, by refocusing economic prediction on the very long term—decades away—and concentrating on the deep factors that will influence that future. That said, I do not presume to be the economic Nostradamus; economics is hardly an exact science, and since economists have at best an imprecise understanding of the world around them, it would be unfair to expect their predictions about the future to be anything other than educated conjecture. Moreover, the further you look into the future, the more difficult prediction becomes; for each moment you extend a forecast, the level of uncertainty rises sharply, since so many more events and actions can interact to change the outcome. Graphs of the forecasts for government budgets, for example, often take the form of a wide-open set of jaws rather than just a single line, because the actual budget could fall anywhere between the two jaws. The area of uncertainty grows with each year added to the projection.

And there is one more complication: predictions about the future may become public, and, when they do, the predictions themselves may affect the future. Economists thus face a kind of uncertainty principle similar to the one proposed by Werner Heisenberg for the physical realm. Heisenberg posited that the more precisely you measured the location of a particle, the more difficult it was to tell where that particle was going, and vice versa. Similarly, the more precisely you predict the future of the global economy, the less likely it may be that the future will conform to your prediction.

This principle need not be disheartening, however, and it certainly does not invalidate the premise of this book. I am fond of recounting a conversation I had with a college roommate over a meal in our dormitory's dining hall. Pointing out the imprecision of economic science, he put it to me that economists' predictions were no better than glorified weather forecasting. In the end I had to agree, but I pointed out to him that a weather forecast that's correct 70 percent of the time is much better than no weather forecast at all.

In fact, a frequent goal of prediction is to alter the future—to warn of impending danger so that it can be avoided. If you're driving a car along a country road and your passenger says, "Watch out for that cow!" then presumably you'll swerve instead of seeing whether your fan belt can slice up some brisket.

If this book does alter the future, not just by allowing its readers to avoid perils and seize opportunities but also by encouraging them to work against those perils and to enhance those opportunities, then it will have more than served its purpose. I hope readers will begin to think about the deep factors that shape the global economy, not just to expand their horizons but to expand their time horizons as well.

PART · I

LIMITS

1

CHINA WILL GET RICHER, AND THEN IT WILL GET POORER AGAIN.

For the past several years, the biggest story in the global economy has been China. During the major part of recorded history, China was the world's great economic power. After a couple of centuries out of the limelight, the Chinese are preparing to be number one again.

China's economic boom has brought hundreds of millions of people out of poverty, often by taking them off their farms and shunting them into China's burgeoning cities, where they now work in factories and other higher-wage occupations. In China's 2000 census, 159 cities could boast a population of a million or more. They are the product of the greatest rural-to-urban migration the world has ever seen, the key to a similarly unprecedented wave of industrialization.

With its economy growing as much as 10 percent per year—even the years of the recent global recession saw rates around 9 percent—China has seemed unstoppable. A 2003 report by Goldman Sachs predicted that China would eclipse the United States as the world's biggest economy in 2041 and continue to grow faster than the United States until at least 2050. In the midst of that growth, the average income of Chinese people would catch up with those of people in many wealthier countries, going from 3 percent of the average American income in 2003—a figure somewhat distorted by exchange rates, to be sure—all the way up to 37 percent in 2050. And according to the predictive models used by the Goldman Sachs team, the Chinese would continue to close the gap after 2050.

The enthusiasm for China has continued in the teeth of the recent crisis in the global economy. Martin Jacques, the author of a book called *When China Rules the World*, published in 2009, has said that China will replace the United States as the world's main superpower. He even thinks Shanghai will overtake New York as a financial center, and the yuan-renminbi, China's currency, will supplant the dollar in world markets.

Considering the deep factors driving China's growth, these forecasts look far too optimistic. China will indeed get richer, relative to other countries, for years to come. But then it will get poorer again, and in all likelihood it will surrender the title of the world's biggest economy just a few years after wresting it from the United States.

IN economics there are few axioms and fewer laws. The science, if it can be called that, lacks the certainty of mathematics and the elegance of physics, which may be why quite a few run-of-the-mill mathematicians and physicists turn out to be excellent economists.

But economics does come close to these other disciplines in its mapping of individual decisions and economic growth. Models of economic growth, in particular, usually look familiar to physicists, as they often appear to mimic the motion of particles influenced by forces like gravity. These models, which became popular during the 1980s and have endured since then, are usually called "neoclassical" because they draw heavily on classical mathematical and statistical techniques developed much earlier, in the 1920s.

From the neoclassical models arose perhaps the only relationship that economics has been able to establish between
the prospects for growth of different countries. This is not to
say that the models gave birth to a law. Rather, they suggested
a relationship that, when tested in the real world, appears to
hold true: convergence.

The idea of convergence began with the simplest models,
in which there was little to distinguish economies from one
another. In these models, it looked as though every economy
was on the same path of growth. Some had a head start, and
they were already wealthy. The others, however, would catch up
to the leaders eventually. In fact, the further behind they were,
the more quickly they would close the gap. As time passed, the
workers in every economy would be heading toward the same
average level of productivity, and thus, in a world of competitive markets, toward the same wages and material standards of
living.

Plenty of observable evidence indicated that this theory
might be right. Countries that lagged far behind the leaders—
the poorest ones—could make dramatic leaps forward by making basic improvements in public health, education, and
infrastructure, which would eventually allow them to move
their people off the land and into cities, where they could take
advantage of the economies of scale implicit in industrial production. Moreover, the laggards could copy technologies from
the leaders rather than having to develop them on their own,
leapfrogging through economic time. As they began to compete
head-to-head with the leaders in the highest-value markets,
however, their progress would naturally slow.

Yet this simple form of convergence didn't seem to be
happening in many parts of the world. African countries, for
example, actually lost ground to the rich West in the second
half of the twentieth century. And some countries that appeared
to be catching up to the West for a few decades, like Japan, hit a
wall before they reached the same standards of living, falling

inexplicably short of the target. Indeed, as the theory of convergence became canonical in economics textbooks during the 1980s, bestselling books predicted that Japan would pass the United States and become the world's greatest economic power. That never happened, and today few economists would predict it ever will.

So economists reexamined the theory of convergence. They decided that the basic idea could still be correct, but with a caveat: countries' living standards could converge in the long term, but only if they had similar sets of economic foundations. These foundations were the deep factors whose importance was easily perceptible yet hard to quantify. Some were immutable, like geography or cultural traditions; landlocked countries could not easily get access to the sea, nor could countries accustomed to autocratic rulers suddenly forget their history. Others, like legal philosophies and the depth of ingrained corruption, could be changed, though only with great effort and over the course of years. Together, these deep factors created the backdrop for all economic activity. The economy could rise and fall with its usual cycle, but the deep factors determined the economy's potential to grow in the very long term, decades or even centuries into the future.

Countries that shared several of these deep factors could be put in the same "convergence club," meaning that the basic dynamic of convergence could be expected to hold for them. Only by changing one or more of the deep factors could a country jump from one club to another, thereby changing its target for living standards and its long-term path of economic growth. In the late twentieth century, Japan hit a wall because it didn't have the same deep factors underpinning its growth as the United States. Its markets weren't as competitive, and the bureaucracy governing its business environment was more cumbersome. It wasn't in the same convergence club and, even at its full potential, couldn't be expected to catch or pass the United States.

This new theory, called "conditional convergence," has

endured in mainstream economics in large part because of the strength of the evidence that supports it. Early calculations showed that, controlling for population growth and the rate of investment in capital goods, per capita income in a sample of 121 countries did appear to converge over time. A later study showed that, conditional on their ability to export, East Asian economies seemed to converge toward similar income levels—those with lower standards of living tended to grow faster. Conditional on having similar economic and political institutions, African countries in the postcolonial period also displayed convergence. These studies divided countries into convergence clubs in different ways—after all, you can slice and dice the world's economies however you want—but the distinguishing characteristics in each club were important enough to influence the members' economic futures.

Until the late 1970s, China was languishing in one of the lower-productivity convergence clubs. The Cultural Revolution had eliminated or literally put out to pasture many of the country's best minds, and China's massive yet ill-conceived industrial mobilizations—backyard steel-smelting, for example—had yielded little fruit. The country was largely shut out of overseas markets through a combination of regulations and the poor quality of its output. Starting after World War II, China had steadily lost ground to its industrializing neighbors. Having chosen a unique set of economic institutions, in which central planning of the economy was mixed with the atomization of industrial production in thousands of villages, China was arguably in a convergence club all its own—and not a very fast-moving one.

That changed when Deng Xiaoping, who began to take over the central posts in the Chinese government after the death of Mao Zedong in 1976, initiated a series of economic reforms. He reached out to foreign leaders, began to open China to overseas markets, allowed more Chinese students to study abroad, and even laid the groundwork for the return of private entrepreneurship. As his regime continued, the state tacitly gave more and more day-to-day control of finance and industry back to the market by allowing private companies to operate and grow, even when their existence seemed to contravene official dictums.

These reforms made a fundamental difference to China's growth, and the productivity of its workers has started to catch up to that of local heavyweights like South Korea and Japan. But is drawing level with South Korea or Japan an attainable goal, or will China come up short, just as Japan did in its pursuit of the United States? The answer will depend on whether China is in the same convergence club as its wealthy neighbors.

And the answer is probably no. Despite the dramatic changes in the Chinese economy since the late 1970s, there are still vast differences between China and wealthier economies that are likely to hold China back. Some of them might be changeable within the next couple of decades, and some of them might not.

Two factors that economists regard as particularly important to convergence in incomes, especially as poor countries close the gap with rich ones, are openness to trade and the ease of starting a business. China has done much to open its markets since Mao's death, but it still has a long way to go. Details of the trade agreements that helped it to join the World Trade Organization in 2001, such as how much its exports can undercut the prices of domestically produced goods in the United States and Europe, are still being disputed today. And though China marched right in when other countries swung open their doors to its cheap manufactured goods, it has not yet opened its own markets to the same extent.

When it comes to opening a business, China ranks even further behind. The World Bank's annual study of environments for entrepreneurs, appropriately called "Doing Business," ranked China 151st out of 181 countries in the category "Starting a Business." The ranking, based on a survey of the experts and businesspeople conducted by the bank, compares the time and money needed to start a small business in different countries, encompassing both the burden of bureaucratic procedures and the legal requirements for financing. In China, an entrepreneur would need to have financial capital on hand amounting to more than 130 percent of the average annual income to start a business. In 91 other economies, from Afghanistan to Zimbabwe (and including heavyweights such as the United States, Japan, and Germany), no such requirement exists. China may be the world's second-biggest economy, but there are very few places in the world where it's more difficult to hang out one's shingle for the first time.

These factors can be fixed. China has a strong central government that can institute new regulations quickly and enforce them with an iron fist. In time, China can become as encouraging an environment for new investment, both by foreigners and by its own people, as any other industrialized country. There are other factors, however, that are not so easy to alter. In the very long term, these factors may turn out to be the most important ones.

THE main determinant of China's very-long-term future will be what the neoclassical model calls "technology." This term doesn't just include the kind of technology you pick up at an electronics superstore. It represents every single factor that determines how people combine their labor with raw materials to create goods and services. It's not just blueprints and recipes, but also the level of corruption, the way managers treat their employees, how the law protects investors, the influence of culture on the competitive climate, how educational traditions affect workers' creativity—you name it, it's in there. These deep factors will determine which convergence club China is in, and it is here that China is likely to fall short.

Confucianism is perhaps the leading influence on Chinese business practices, or at least the single factor that most distinguishes Chinese practices from those of other countries. The teachings of Confucius date back centuries, and they are deeply ingrained in Chinese society. The Chinese government has even embraced them in recent decades alongside its official communist ideology; in 1996 the *People's Daily*, China's influential state newspaper, called for an understanding of Confucianism's "precious business philosophies." Yet some of its central tenets, though they may have benefits at the social level, are not necessarily conducive to economic growth.

Confucian ethics teach that one should value the collective over the individual. Though Confucius himself did not view the supremacy of the collective as a justification for conformism—he was more of the opinion that individuals could shine within the collective, as long as the collective remained harmonious—his ideas became distorted in modern China. According to Daniel Bell, a scholar of Chinese philosophy at Tsinghua University in Beijing, Confucianism was melded with Chinese authorities' legalistic inclinations to lend a legitimizing cultural resonance to their strict imposition of law and order. A second and related tenet of Confucianism could be termed propriety, or an adherence to ceremony or tradition; it encompasses the "respect for elders" that is a hallmark of many East Asian civilizations. In Confucianism, this deference belongs not just in family relationships but also between ruler and subject, master and servant, and employer and employee.

Together, these tenets of Confucianism—and the way they have been interpreted by the Chinese authorities in recent times—have helped to maintain rigid hierarchies in Chinese businesses. Even Confucius, Bell concedes, did not believe that young people should engage in critical thinking. First they had to learn the teachings of their elders. They had to attain more seniority within the collective before they could begin to challenge established ideas and innovate.

These hierarchies within the collective can be problematic in a mature economy. As the management researchers Yuan Fang and Chris Hall point out, when Chinese managers make decisions, the consequences of those decisions must cascade down through many levels of corporate hierarchy, perhaps being diluted along the way; this time-consuming process can reduce a company's ability to react quickly to changing business conditions. Meanwhile, incompetent managers can stay in their jobs simply because of their seniority. The ideas of junior workers are rarely implemented, even if they have the temerity to raise their voices, because their proposals get stuck on the way up the chain of command. In a country where starting a new business is difficult, this problem is exacerbated; young workers frustrated with the Chinese system might try to emigrate rather than strike out on their own as entrepreneurs.

The combination of these two tenets is implicit in the bulk of large Chinese firms, because the government—the ultimate "elder" that supposedly represents the collective—has a controlling interest. It is not always a healthy interest. Maximizing profits is not necessarily the government's only goal; if it were, the government would sell its interest in companies when doing so would yield the biggest payoff. Research shows that government-dominated companies pay lower dividends and have less healthy cash flow. The same is true for companies with complex, hierarchical ownership structures. Publicly traded Chinese companies can have as many as five classes of shares, while American companies rarely have more than two or three.

One other cultural current runs just as deeply as Confucianism. Through books, films, and classes, Chinese people learn a very particular story of the birth of their nation, in which the great struggle through the millennia has been to unite the enormous landmass and diverse ethnicities of China into one nation. Those who sought to carve China into smaller kingdoms are usually the villains; those who sought to unite it are the heroes. Those heroes are often merciless and violent, like the Qin emperor Shi Huang, who cut a bloody swath across China with armies of tens of thousands of men as he united seven kingdoms into one empire in the third century B.C. That empire eventually fell apart, but the next rulers to unite China—the Sui—were just as ruthless. And so the story goes, all the way up to and including Mao. The message is clear: to be united and realize the dreams of a great Chinese nation, the Chinese people need strong rulers who brook little dissent.

The message carries through to the boardrooms of Chinese companies, which tend to concentrate the instruments of power in the hands of a single strongman who unites the three most important roles in the company: chief executive, chairman of the board, and representative of the Chinese Communist Party. The boss thereby represents the interests of the government, which is often the biggest stakeholder, and common shareholders are marginalized.

Not surprisingly, the narrative of uniting disparate kingdoms to form a single, stronger empire also has echoes in the growth strategy of Chinese companies. Some of the biggest, like the appliance maker Haier, have grown at astonishing rates by gobbling up their smaller competitors. Doing so can generate economies of scale and lower prices for consumers. But if one company becomes the unchallenged industry leader, then that company will have little incentive to innovate or cater to changing preferences.

Making China's business environment even more challenging is a pervasive lack of transparency. China's complex bureaucracy has allowed corruption to become entrenched, and the government has been known to use the legal system to bully foreign companies. Economic data are regularly revised and contested; a recent video series presented by *The Atlantic* pointed out that even estimates of the country's population vary by hundreds of millions of people. In part because of these factors, business negotiations in China tend to be based more on personal relationships and trust than on numbers and contracts.

The rhetoric of some Western politicians suggests they believe that China will eventually embrace democracy and transparency, perhaps after a long period of economic opening. Yet that will not necessarily change all of the deep factors that are limiting China's growth; the links between political institutions and the economic climate are not always so strong. For example, South Korea, despite becoming a democracy, still has a very Confucian culture with the attendant repercussions for innovation and corporate hierarchies. Russia, another large country long governed by a strong central authority (be it a tsar, Joseph Stalin, or Vladimir Putin), essentially tried democracy and rejected it over the past twenty years; corruption and government strong-arming of foreign companies continue unabated. Sweden, for decades a democratic country, maintained heavy state involvement in the economy until a decade ago.

It may be a stretch, therefore, to assume that China's hierarchies will flatten out, or that its government will substantially reduce its presence in many sectors of the Chinese economy, a presence that can crowd out private ventures and deter foreign investment. Indeed, three decades after its "open-door policy" began, China's government is still heavily involved in virtually all of its big companies. This involvement amounts to actual ownership and control, in contrast to the government-led coordination and protections for private companies that helped industries grow in South Korea, Japan, and Taiwan during the twentieth century.

In addition, the government is unlikely to rein in the massive bureaucracy that allows it to maintain control of municipalities thousands of miles from Beijing, even though that very bureaucracy is often what stands in the way of new businesses. It may also be reluctant to increase the transparency of its legal system, since that same lack of transparency can be used to hamper and curtail the activities of foreign companies at the government's whim.

All of these factors will combine to lower the target for material living standards in China. To put it more technically, they reduce the level of per capita income toward which China is converging; with these factors in place, China simply is not in the same convergence club as the United States. More likely, it is in a club along with other nations that share at least some of its cultural grounding, legal framework, history of state involvement in the economy, industrialization patterns and climate, perhaps including Vietnam and Kazakhstan. As these examples suggest, countries do not have to be the same size to be in the same convergence club. The deep factors that underpin economic growth set the achievable limits for material living standards; those limits can be similar in countries of various sizes.

This is not to say that China is incapable of progress. One study completed in 1999 suggested that younger managers in Chinese companies were more individualistic than those of previous generations, a characteristic that could help to promote innovation in the long term. By now many of those young managers are undoubtedly in positions of power. But there are simply too many deeply ingrained differences for China's people to attain the same incomes as their Western counterparts at the end of its current growth spurt. Those incomes ultimately depend on workers' productivity; you are paid for what you produce. Chinese workers, even with access to the latest gadgets and manufacturing techniques, cannot be as productive as American or European workers if they do not have the same entrepreneurial opportunities, a transparent regulatory framework, strong legal protections, efficient corporate structures, and the ability to innovate.

FIXING the target for material living standards, however, says little about the speed of growth. Generally, economists believe that countries converge faster when they are further away from their targets—that is, when their incomes are much lower than incomes in the economies that lead their convergence clubs. The 2003 Goldman Sachs report suggested that China's growth was still pretty far from stabilizing, even after a quarter-century of reform by Deng and his successors, with at least four decades to go before the economy caught up to the leaders. Yet, looking carefully at China's history and that of other rapidly developing countries, it seems likely that China will stabilize sooner, with many fewer years of rapid growth in the interim.

China has been moving through the stages of modern economic growth faster than any other large economy ever has. When Deng took over, it looked like a country at the very beginnings of industrialization, with the vast majority of its population still engaged in agriculture. Most of those farmers lived at the subsistence level, growing just enough crops to feed their families. It was a very poor country.

In a mere three decades, China has transformed itself into a middle-income country and an industrial powerhouse. A major part of this transformation has been China's ability to catch up to wealthier nations by copying technology, sometimes even using joint ventures to steal production techniques from foreign partners. But those technologies would have been useless without the vast wave of urbanization that has taken workers off their farms and into China's ever-growing cities to produce cheap manufactured goods for the whole world.

It is hardly surprising that convergence and urbanization tend to go hand in hand. Once the opportunities in the city are no better than those in the country—that is, once the factories become saturated with labor and agriculture has been made as efficient as it possibly can be—urbanization naturally tapers off. The United States, for example, became a manufacturing hub for the world around the turn of the twentieth century. It reached its economic maturity toward the end of the 1960s, as the space race and the postwar brain drain from Europe provided the impetus and the wherewithal to turn a manufacturing superpower into a champion of technology and high-value services.

In 1910, the Census of the United States found 46 percent of the American population living in urban areas, with their numbers having grown by about 3 percent per year over the previous decade. From the 1910s through the 1950s, the urban population of the United States grew by about 2 percent per year, until about two-thirds of Americans were living in cities. Then, in the 1960s and 1970s, urbanization in the United States slowed until the cities were growing at about the same rate as the overall population.

In 2008, China's cities accounted for 43 percent of its total population, and the urban population was growing by a little less than 3 percent per year. And there were other parallels with the United States in 1910. The rash of consumer goods scandals that hit China in this decade echoed the outrage of Americans upon reading *The Jungle*, Upton Sinclair's muckraking 1906 novel about the meatpacking industry in Chicago. Americans then campaigned for better working conditions as well as for safer products, just as Chinese laborers—especially internal migrants—are doing now. Both countries' workers were getting wealthier, forming a new urban middle class, and were beginning to assert their rights as workers and consumers.

So, does this mean that China can expect five or six decades of strong growth until it reaches its maturity? Not necessarily. For one thing, as discussed above, it may not be heading toward as high a target for living standards as the United States was. The path may be similar, but that does not mean the destination is the same.

Moreover, urbanization now is not the same as urbanization then. Advances in farming technology can push Chinese workers off their farms without sacrificing crop production. Cities to house those workers can be constructed more rapidly than ever before. Globalized markets for goods and services along with "just-in-time" supply chains allow opportunities to be matched with workers and resources more rapidly than ever. If anything, China's urbanization should take much less time than that of the United States. This may explain China's current breakneck pace of economic growth: it's faster than the economic growth in the United States in the peak years of urbanization—about 10 percent per year, adjusted for inflation, compared to 7 percent in the United States—and the reason may be that the whole process is being compressed into a shorter period.

It's also possible that China won't urbanize to the extent that the United States has. Again, consider the example of Japan. Back in the early 1950s, Japan had an urban-to-rural population ratio like China's ratio today. By 1975, more than three-quarters of Japan's population was living in cities, a proportion that barely changed at all for a quarter of a century. Japan's urbanization and its rapid economic growth seemed to be over until the first decade of the twenty-first century, when a new urbanization wave—perhaps one that will at last help Japan to catch up a little more to the United States and Western Europe—finally began.

Because of these factors, China may only have three or four decades of fast growth left. As it nears its target for average incomes—a target likely to be lower than that of the world's economic pacesetters—its waves of leapfrog engineering and mass urbanization will run out of steam, and it will settle down into a steady growth pattern, as almost all of the world's major industrialized economies already have. The deep factors detailed above imply that, when this finally happens, China's average incomes are unlikely to be as high as those in the West or even those in South Korea and Japan. Then the question will become whether the average growth rate of China's economy will be high enough to keep it among the leaders, like the United States.

In the neoclassical model, only economies with equivalent "technology"—the catchall variable for the deep factors and everything else—can expand at the same rate when they settle into their steady growth pattern. If China's "technology" is inferior for the purposes of economic growth, then it will begin to lose ground. In other words, its average incomes will start to fall behind those of the world's economic pacesetters. The Chinese people, having become substantially richer relative to the rest of the world, will slowly become poorer again.

But what does this mean for China's economic might? Average incomes are a measure of material living standards, but they don't say anything about the power of an economy to buy up resources, dominate markets, and mobilize for huge projects like wars and space exploration. To extend the prediction, the missing ingredient is the growth of China's population, and specifically the labor force.

There, the news is not good. A report published in 2007 by the International Labor Organization stated that China was the fastest-aging country in history. The report showed that the famous "one-child policy" instituted by Beijing in 1979, though not uniformly enforced, had truly taken hold; the population's growth rate had fallen to just under 0.7 percent per year. The overall population grew by just 0.5 percent in 2008, the last year for which government statistics were available at the time of this writing. According to estimates by the United Nations, China's working-age population—people between fifteen and fifty-nine years of age—will fall from 67 percent of the total population in 2005 to just 54 percent in 2050.

Japan and some countries in Europe will also see substantial shrinkage in their labor forces and even their entire populations. But the working-age population in the United States will only dip from 62 percent of the total in 2005 to 56 percent in 2050—less than half the drop in China—if current trends in fertility and immigration hold. This difference will only amplify differences in the growth rates of average incomes, meaning that China's economic might will dwindle even more rapidly than its material living standards fall behind those of the United States.

So what does all this mean? First, consider the conventional wisdom. The Goldman Sachs report predicted that China would overtake the United States as the world's biggest economy in 2041 and would continue to widen the gap for many years afterward. In 2048, the amount by which China extended its lead every year would slowly begin to fall, in percentage terms, but only by a tiny amount each year.

Now, consider an alternative scenario that encompasses the points made earlier in this chapter, namely that (1) China is not converging to the same living standards as the world's wealthiest nations, (2) China's economic growth will stabilize sooner than expected, and (3) China's long-term economic growth rate will be lower than those of the world's established economic leaders. A reasonable prediction might be that China's growth will stabilize by 2050 at the latest, having grown more slowly than Goldman Sachs predicted; its population will grow no faster than that of the United States; and its long-term growth rate in average incomes will be slightly lower than that of the United States, say 1.5 percent versus 2 percent. Under these conditions, China may just manage to pass the United States and become the world's biggest economy. But it will hold on to the title for only a few years before the United States, growing more quickly in both population and the productivity of its workers, passes China again.

As a result, investors and entrepreneurs who have seen unlimited potential in China will be sorely disappointed. With lower material living standards, Chinese people will never be able to buy as many goods and services as their wealthier counterparts in the United States and Europe. The Chinese market will be immense, but it will not eclipse the world's other major economies. Moreover, the risk to shareholders and creditors implied by corruption, lack of transparency, and the Chinese political system will no longer be offset by the reward of huge profits. The fad for Chinese securities will slowly but surely peter out. In the long march of economic history, China's moment will be impressive, but brief.

AS the neoclassical model went mainstream, some economists tried to improve it by allowing technology to be generated internally, rather than just determined by immutable historical factors. Undoubtedly, this can happen; when an economy experiences a rush of new investment, for example, some of that money usually goes into research and development. But no amount of new capital will change a legal system, nor will it change the doctrines that an economy's people have looked to for guidance over thousands of years.

This is not to say that China is doomed to inferior economic growth and living standards forever. Even the most deeply ingrained traditions can change over the course of decades, or in a shorter period of time if disruptive or revolutionary forces are in play. In Eastern Europe, for example, the collapse of state socialism and the Soviet bloc left several countries with a blank slate. They held on to their cultures, but they were free to choose some of the bedrock institutions of their economies all over again. As the next chapter explains, their choices might have some very far-reaching consequences.

2

THE EUROPEAN UNION WILL DISINTEGRATE AS AN ECONOMIC ENTITY.

At present, the biggest economy in the world is not the United States; it is the European Union. In fact, the Union's annual production of goods and services is almost as valuable as those of the United States and China put together. This is the culmination of a remarkable success story, despite recent troubles. Two decades after the fall of the Berlin Wall, the European Union has become a twenty-seven-country bloc with a population of half a billion people and roughly a third of the world's gross domestic product. It has chosen its first president and deepened its internal economic links, which include free trade, free migration across national borders within the bloc, a shared competition policy, and a single currency—the euro—in use in sixteen of its member countries. In the future, we may look back at this moment as the peak of the European Union's unity and importance as an economic entity. The coming decades will make holding the economic union together increasingly difficult, until, inevitably, it will start to fall apart.

When that happens, the repercussions will be felt around the world. Companies that invested in the Union expecting that it would eventually become one borderless market will have to temper their long-term hopes of easier sales, smoother logistics, transparent hiring, and lower production costs. Gains from trade will be left on the table, economic growth will fall short of potential, and those losses will filter through to the rest of the world via lower spending on imports and less investment abroad by Europeans. In addition, central banks that were diversifying their reserves away from dollars and toward the euro will have to reconsider if not completely reverse that position. The dollar will strengthen, making it more difficult to close the enormous trade deficits that the United States built up over the past decade. In sum, the disintegration of the European Union as an economic entity will unleash destabilizing forces in the short term and leave the world poorer in the long term. A splendid idea in principle, the Union will have lasted less than a century.

The Union's first incarnation, the European Coal and Steel Community of 1951, had one overarching goal: to create economic links between the main powers on the continent that would preempt another devastating war. The group included Belgium, Germany, France, Italy, Luxembourg, and the Netherlands, all battlegrounds in both world wars. They hoped to bind together their economic fortunes as a means of keeping the peace, the logic being that if these essential industries were under joint control, then no single country would be able to mobilize for war. Within a few years, the six members added political links to economic ones by setting up the precursors to the European Commission and the European Parliament, the central institutions that run the Union today. As this integration intensified, more countries joined: Denmark, Ireland, and the United Kingdom in 1973, and then Greece, Spain, and Portugal in the 1980s. Austria, Finland, and Sweden became members in 1995. Eight former Soviet republics and satellite states joined in 2004 along with Malta and Cyprus, and Romania and Bulgaria finally qualified in 2007.

Throughout this process, decisions about membership always took into account a combination of economic and security-related concerns. The early members certainly courted the post-Soviet countries with the goal of removing them from Russia's sphere of influence, but those countries also sought membership on their own as a way to access the huge export and investment markets in the West. The hope was also that, with time, the newer members would develop into economically mature, democratic countries in the original members' own images.

Neither the original members nor the newer ones made up a homogeneous group, however. Even among the original members, there were vast gaps in levels of corruption, the ease of doing business, economic freedom, budget positions, future fiscal liabilities, and economic cycles. In theory, the Union was supposed to eliminate these differences as commerce and competition among the member states made them decreasingly tenable. A country with a persistent corruption problem or a burdensome bureaucracy would have to reform as it saw businesses locating and investing in its neighbors rather than within its borders. Trade and migration between the members would eventually synchronize their economic cycles.

Yet this has not happened. Even in the euro area, where the use of a common currency and monetary policy was supposed to bring the members into economic lockstep—meaning their economies would follow the same cycle, entering booms and busts at roughly the same time—the divergence continues. For example, consider Greece and Italy, neighbors that both use the euro. Despite the crisis in 2008, the Greek economy expanded by 2.9 percent, adjusted for inflation. Next door in Italy, the economy shrank by 1.0 percent. By adopting the euro, these countries had delegated their monetary policy to the European Central Bank in Frankfurt, yet no single monetary policy could have been appropriate for both of them in 2008; one was in a boom, the other in a recession. High short-term interest rates might have helped to quell inflation of over 4.0 percent in Greece, but they would have inflicted even greater pain on Italy by drying up credit there. By contrast, low short-term interest rates, though they might have helped Italy to recover, would have threatened to overheat the Greek economy.

Indeed, it was hard to decipher exactly what kind of policy the bankers in Frankfurt were trying to implement in 2008. They began with their benchmark short-term interest rate at 3.00 percent, raised it to 3.25 percent on July 9, lowered it to 2.75 percent on October 8, immediately reversed themselves by raising the rate back to 3.25 percent on October 9, then lowered it back to 2.75 percent on November 12, and finally lowered it to 2.00 percent on December 10. By that time, the global financial crisis had been in full swing for months, with Lehman Brothers having filed for bankruptcy on September 14.

Clearly, finding any sort of middle path has not been an easy task for economic policymakers in the European Union. And the newer members that joined the Union in 2004 and 2007 have even less in common than Italy and Greece, putting aside the state-socialist past that most of them share. The fall of communism gave them a chance to choose a new set of institutions on which to base their societies, and from an economic perspective, some chose better than others.

Estonia, renowned for its all-electronic banking system, currently ranks 24th out of 183 countries in the World Bank's survey on the ease of doing business; the Czech Republic sits fifty places further down at number 74. (Down at 109 is Greece, the worst place to do business in the entire European Union.) As in China, starting a business in the Czech Republic is anything but easy; it ranks 113th out of 183 countries, with costs to entrepreneurs of almost 10 percent of the average annual income, and about 30 percent of average annual income required by law as start-up capital. Closing a business isn't easy, either. The time needed to wind down a company averages over six years, and investors may recover only 20 cents on the dollar, compared to three years and almost 40 cents on the dollar in Estonia.

Though the European Union requires countries to reduce corruption before becoming members, its prevalence also varies widely within the group. According to Transparency International, Slovenia is the 26th least-corrupt country in the world, but Bulgaria ranks down in the 70s. These results are based on surveys of people who do business in the two countries and analyses by outside organizations like the Economist Intelligence Unit. They encounter less graft in Slovenia; in Bulgaria, organized crime and corruption in politics are still pervasive.

The makeup of the economies of the post-Soviet countries can be vastly different, too, from Romania, where almost 30 percent of the population works in agriculture, to Slovakia, where just 4 percent does. Hungary's exports amount to more than half of its gross domestic product; in Latvia, exports are only a third. There is no synchronicity here, either; Lithuania's economy grew by 3.1 percent in the crisis year of 2008, while its neighbor Latvia's shrank by 4.6 percent.

Differences between the members haven't been the only problem for economic policy in the European Union. As a whole, the members haven't even been able to abide by the economic rules they set for themselves via the Stability and Growth Pact, most recently codified in 2005. Under that treaty, the Union's members agreed to keep budget deficits low in an effort to minimize internal economic hiccups. Yet from the beginning, even before the global economic crisis of 2008, countries large and small had trouble holding to the deficit limit of 3 percent of gross domestic product. Penalties for breaking the rules were not automatic and practically negligible: countries simply had to deposit money with the European Union's administration for a couple of years, during which they could correct the imbalance—and this only if the Union's ruling council so ordered. The crisis, when it did come, made the pact practically irrelevant, because so many members incurred heavy deficits as they spent borrowed money to stimulate their economies.

The onset of the global economic crisis provided the first warning shot that the economic bonds within the European Union might not have been as strong as they once appeared. Italy was struggling with a deep recession in early 2008, yet even as late as July of that year, the European Central Bank was actually raising short-term interest rates. The failure to accommodate led several experts and pundits to suggest that Italy or other troubled countries like Greece and Spain might exit the euro area—something no country had ever done— and return to an independent currency. Some scholars insisted that the benefits of being inside the euro area (such as protection from exchange rate volatility) and the costs of leaving (in terms of both logistics and reputation in the financial markets) made dropping the common currency a nonstarter. But in March 2008, the financial prediction website Intrade began taking bets on whether any country would drop the euro by the end of 2010. At the height of the crisis, the odds reached a high of 40 percent.

Then, as the crisis appeared to be receding in early 2010, Greece's new government revealed the depth of the country's fiscal problems. Its books had been cooked for years, and the country was having trouble finding enough money to pay the interest on its debts. With the country at risk of default—that is, of failing to pay the investors who held bonds the interest they had been promised—the country was under enormous pressure to drop the euro as its currency and reinstate the drachma. Investors were fleeing Greece, but the government, without control of the currency, was hamstrung. The country needed a looser monetary policy consisting of lower interest rates and a lower exchange rate (achieved essentially by printing money) to create some inflation. With inflation in prices for goods and services, the value in real terms of Greece's debt would drop; as anyone with a mortgage or a car loan knows, inflation is the borrower's friend. Moreover, a little inflation might help to spur demand in the Greek economy, and a lower exchange rate would make Greek exports more attractive to the rest of the world.

But Greece was in the euro area, and so control of its interest and exchange rates was in the hands of the European Central Bank in Frankfurt. Would Frankfurt apply the policies Greece needed to the euro area as a whole? It seemed unlikely, since Greece represented less than 4 percent of the euro area's population. So, if monetary policy could not provide any succor, Greece would need fiscal help. This was a matter of extreme importance. If the rest of the European Union didn't come to Greece's rescue, it would make investors think twice about lending money to other countries in the euro area with heavy debt burdens, like Portugal and Spain. Yet helping Greece to pay its debts by virtue of its membership in the euro area and the European Union would be in direct contravention of Article 104b of the Union's Maastricht Treaty of 1992, which begins, "The Community shall not be liable for or assume the commitments of central governments."

Perhaps more important, if the European Union were going to back Greece, then other members of the euro area might feel free to run up big debts of their own. With the euro area heading toward deeper indebtedness, the currency's value would be undermined—what if the European Central Bank decided it had to cut interest rates and devalue, trying to stimulate the whole area so that it could pay its debts, just like Greece in the scenario above? Central banks that had begun diversifying their reserves away from dollars (like the People's Bank of China) would have to reconsider. Foreigners who had invested in stocks and bonds from the euro area would see the values of their portfolios decline, even if the companies behind them kept earning profits.

Despite these concerns, the European Union's leaders

decided that the risk of letting Greece default was unacceptable. They offered low-interest loans of up to $105 billion to
their struggling ally—a staggering amount for a country whose
annual gross domestic product was only about $350 billion.
The International Monetary Fund, whose board is dominated
by the European Union and the United States, offered another
$40 billion on even more favorable terms. Treaty or no, Greece
was considered too big, or at least too interconnected, to fail.

THE aftermath of the global financial crisis of 2008 had pushed
the European Union to the breaking point as an economic
entity. But to be fair, the European Union was showing one
important sign of convergence: five years into the Union's biggest expansion, the poorer countries were catching up to the
richer ones in terms of material living standards. In 2007, the
last year before the crisis, average economic growth in the first
fifteen countries to join the Union was 3.2 percent, compared
to 6.5 percent in the last twelve. In fact, eight out of the last
twelve countries to join enjoyed higher growth than all fifteen
of the older members.

   This came as little surprise, given the economic situation of
the newer members. Wages were lower in Eastern Europe, and
jobs in both manufacturing and services were moving there
by the thousands, both from Western Europe and from the
United States. The crops and raw materials that the newer
members produced could also sell freely at a higher price in
the West and in countries with which the European Union
had trade agreements. The improvements in institutions and
transparency that the newer members did make in order to
accede to the Union were helping them to attract new investment, too.

   Still, the fact that many of those newer members did not
make deeper economic reforms will impose limits on their
rapid growth. They did make a onetime jump to fulfill the cri-

teria for entry to the Union: creating market economies with a view toward joining the euro area, bringing their laws into line with the European Union's existing legislation, and fighting corruption in their political systems. But since they entered, they have not made much progress, and some countries have even regressed.

Lithuania and Slovakia were ranked as the 17th and 18th easiest economies for doing business by the World Bank in 2004; as of this writing, they sit in 26th and 42nd places, respectively. According to the experts and businesspeople surveyed, starting a business became substantially more difficult in both countries, and enforcing contracts also became more difficult in Slovakia. Bulgaria slipped from 64th to 72nd in the Corruption Perceptions Index between 2007 and 2008. The backsliding had tangible causes. At the 13th International Anti-Corruption Conference, in Athens in 2008, representatives of the European Commission (the Union's administrative branch) said that anticorruption agencies set up to prepare countries like Bulgaria for accession to the Union had been gutted or even disbanded after membership was secured.

The newer members do have one advantage over the older ones, though. The long-term risks they are facing, in terms of debts and demographically driven liabilities, are generally much smaller than those of the older members. Even before the economic crisis of 2008, several of the older members had taken on large public debts—as much as 104 percent of gross domestic product in Italy and 89 percent in Greece. After the crisis, the situation worsened; Italy's debt burden grew to 115 percent of gross domestic product in 2009, and Greece's debt hit 113 percent. Even some of the countries that didn't make news started to enter dangerous territory: Belgium hit 99 percent, and France, Hungary, Germany, and Portugal were all between 70 and 80 percent.

Several countries will see their populations age significantly over the next few decades, too. Smaller cohorts of workers will be asked to pay the pensions and benefits of bigger cohorts of retirees. In Italy, the ratio of people aged sixty-five or over to those in the prime working years (between twenty-five and sixty-four) will reach 69 percent in 2040, according to the U.S. Census Bureau's projections, compared to 36 percent in 2009. Consider what that means in concrete terms: for every retiree being supported by a worker's taxes today, there will be two in 2040. The ratio may also rise sharply in other countries, to 65 percent in Spain and 64 percent in both Germany and Austria.

There will be no easy way to close these gaps. Retirement ages will have to rise, benefits will have to fall, taxes will have to increase, governments will have to issue more debt, or, more likely, some combination of all of these will occur. Workers confronted by these prospects will start to look for other places to live. When they leave, taking their incomes with them, tax revenues will fall and the gaps will widen even further. The affected countries will end up in fiscal death spirals, with labor forces shrinking and deficits ballooning from year to year. Eventually, they will have to default on their obligations. By this time, their membership in the euro area and their participation in the European Union's other economic treaties will be untenable. Their rising debts, denominated in euros, will pose a threat to the value of the currency, since there will be pressure on the European Central Bank to loosen monetary policy and allow inflation to gradually lower the value of the debt in real terms. Maintaining fiscal discipline as specified by the Stability and Growth Pact will be unacceptable, as it would likely result in a massive cutback in public services and an epidemic of poverty.

As a result of these economic changes, the societies of these countries will become less stable. The deal between generations that keeps most pension systems going—each generation pays for the next, on the assumption that it will also benefit from the same arrangement when it retires—will have broken down. Retirees will expect their governments to keep their promises, but workers will resent having to pay for benefits when their own pensions are hardly secure. Unemployment will rise as governments reduce the rolls of public employees and over-whelm the credit markets with their borrowing, crowding out private enterprises.

Some countries in the European Union will survive these problems not just because of more favorable debt and demo-graphic positions, but also because of their economic potential. Gauged by their levels of corruption, the ease of doing busi-ness, and the breadth of economic freedom, a few countries stand apart from the rest. When citizens of the Union begin looking for better places to live and work, they will naturally gravitate toward these countries.

So, which countries are which? One way to find out is by combining the indexes and figures we've discussed in a new meta-analysis that divides the countries into four distinct groups, along the axes of long-term economic potential and long-term economic risk. (See the chart on page 40.) The index of poten-tial is a simple average of the countries' most recent scores in the World Bank's Doing Business survey (the bank was kind enough to provide percentile scores in lieu of rankings), Trans-parency International's Corruption Perceptions Index, and the Heritage Foundation's Index of Economic Freedom. The index of risk is a scaled average of two figures: the ratio of sixty-five-plus citizens to working-age citizens in 2040 as predicted by the U.S. Census Bureau (based on births to date and trends in fer-tility and immigration), and the ratio of debt to gross domestic product. These are only a few of the variables that will determine these countries' futures, but they do illustrate some important differences.

The results are startlingly uniform. In the top-right quad-rant are the countries with lowest risk and highest potential. These are seven of the northernmost countries in the Union (with the United Kingdom just above the X axis), and all but Luxembourg are endowed with essentially Anglo-Saxon or

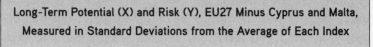

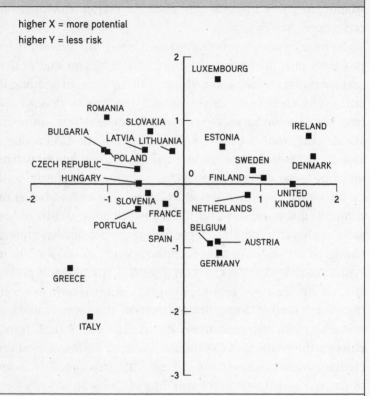

SOURCES: U.S. Central Intelligence Agency *World Factbook 2010*, U.S. Census Bureau *International Data Base*, World Bank *Doing Business 2010*, Transparency International *Corruption Perceptions Index 2009*, Heritage Foundation *Index of Economic Freedom 2010*

Scandinavian legal traditions. The Scandinavian civil law system is probably the closest to common law in its style of jurisprudence of all the civil law systems in Europe. Estonia's post-Soviet choices brought it the closest to the United States and United Kingdom of all the former socialist republics and satellites. (Perhaps not surprisingly, the United States would sit just northwest of Ireland on this chart.)

With Estonia aside, all eight of the nine other post-Soviet members of the European Union find themselves in the top-left quadrant (with Hungary just above the X axis): low long-term risk, but low long-term potential as well. They will continue to catch up to their Western neighbors in technology, productivity, and wages, but they probably won't match them. Eventually, they will settle into a more moderate cycle of growth.

Meanwhile, in the bottom-left quadrant, sit all the southernmost countries not already mentioned, including Slovenia; every single one has territory south of the 46th Parallel, and all but Greece are part of a contiguous landmass. As detailed above, the plights of Greece and Italy are particularly worrying. Finally, in the bottom-right quadrant, there are the wild cards. Austria, Belgium, Germany, and the Netherlands, which together form one contiguous mass of neighbors, have moderately high levels of long-term risk but also more potential than the southerners.

That the distinctions here are almost entirely geographic (and a little bit cultural) should worry the folks in Brussels. If the problem children of the European Union were scattered around its wide expanse, it would be more difficult for the bloc to become segmented along economic lines. Yet the four quadrants are almost entirely separated by geography as well as by risk and potential.

These differences could be lessened by the economic integration that the European Union will achieve under the momentum that it has already accumulated. In the past decade, trade between the countries that now make up the Union has increased by more than 75 percent. In their first two years in the bloc, Bulgaria and Romania both saw their intra-Union trade rise by about 30 percent. Migration flows from East to West have also been dramatic in some cases (from Poland into the United Kingdom) if moderate in others (from Hungary, to Sweden). There is no doubt that the economic fortunes of the European Union's members are becoming more closely intertwined, if not synchronized. The problem is that this trend may be moving too slowly to create much solidarity between them.

It is easy to imagine that the northwestern, non-Latin nations of the European Union would begin to sense, in a couple of decades, that their fellow members were not quite holding up their end of the economic bargain. At first, this sensation would not necessarily result in policy changes. The commercial and financial links between the northwestern countries might simply continue to intensify while the other members of the Union were progressively excluded. As the southern and eastern countries began to fall behind in living standards and run afoul of the economic treaties, however, the northwestern countries would find themselves in the same boat, trying not to be dragged down by the laggards. This tension would have very real effects.

Right now, the West subsidizes the East to the tune of nine billion euros each year; in other words, if we add up all the taxes and subsidies paid and received by the member countries, the East ends up with a positive balance—and every single post-Soviet country is in the net receivers' column. That figure of nine billion euros is not very big in the grand scheme of things, however. Among the post-Soviet countries, the biggest subsidy in proportional terms goes to Lithuania, which received a bump worth a little more than 2 percent of its gross domestic product in 2008. The subsidies would have to rise substantially to allow the eastern countries to continue closing the gap in living standards with the West. As the Union begins to segment economically, the enthusiasm for such payments will be limited at best.

The result will be a very different European Union. The political agreements that bind the countries together would remain in force; they would still pursue foreign policy interests together and be subject to the same laws under the European Court of Justice. But some of the existing economic agreements would be voided (like the Stability and Growth Pact) or scaled back (like the monetary union of the euro area), and new agreements would not necessarily cover all of the members. Half, perhaps more, of the countries in the European Union would only have second-class membership.

At this point, external factors might come into play. Seeing that its former satellites are being marginalized within the European Union, Russia might try to cultivate stronger ties with these countries and eventually restore them to its sphere of influence. The United States might also take advantage of the opportunity to deepen its relationships with the marginalized countries in the south and east of Europe as a counterweight to the other countries, like France and Germany, which have at times stood in the way of American foreign policy goals. This already happened during the administration of George W. Bush, when Italy, Poland, and Romania became some of the firmest European allies in its war on terror. If an administration with a similar orientation were to come to power in Washington, it could happen again.

The political shifts arising from economic eventualities would only increase tensions within the union. Eventually, some of the poorer members may decide that they need to strike out on their own to achieve their economic goals. Their priorities in trade, for example, will be different from those of some of their fellow members, and they may not want to negotiate as a bloc anymore. Consider the ongoing negotiations at the World Trade Organization: Germany and France want to pry open foreign markets for their insurance, real estate, and financial services firms. To Romania and Bulgaria, those goals are not terribly important, but it is important for these countries to export manufactured goods and crops. Yet Germany and France's positions carry much more weight when the European Union's representatives sit down at the bargaining table. Romania, Bulgaria, and other countries in the East will be desperate for economic growth. They won't want to give up access to the markets in the West, but they won't want to rely on the West to represent them, either.

THAT is the scenario if the forces now in motion are allowed to take their course. Because these predictions cover such a long period of time, however, there is room to maneuver. Two or three decades are enough to make major changes in an economy, whether in its underlying institutions or in long-term investments such as basic research, education, and infrastructure. To do these things, a country needs political will and political continuity. The people and leaders need to perceive the risks, grasp the opportunities, and commit to maintaining the same posture even as the parties in power change.

A country cannot, for example, improve the skills of its workforce by investing in education for just a few years. It must invest in education for a full sixteen years to see one cohort all the way through school and university. Nor can a country invest in basic research and technology for just a few years. Pathbreaking scientific projects take years to develop and, once major discoveries have been made, many more years—often a decade or two—are needed to turn them into commercially viable products. But in both cases, the returns are enormous.

Maintaining this kind of patience and consistency is not easy, especially when the current generations of citizens must make sacrifices to give their successors a better future. It is also difficult when politicians have short time horizons or are insecure in their posts; a prime minister leading a fragile coalition might decide that she needs a series of quick wins to consolidate her power rather than making costly reforms that will only pay off in the distant future. Countries where there are frequent changes in leadership will probably have the hardest time reforming their economies and improving their fiscal situations, assuming they have the political will to do so.

If we take a fifteen-year period going back to January 1, 1995 (and no further, so that we give the post-Soviet countries a few years after the fall of the Berlin Wall to organize themselves), the number of changes in heads of government experienced by the European Union countries in the chart on page 40 was as follows:

12	Lithuania
10	Latvia
9	Romania
7	Czech Republic, Italy
6	Bulgaria, Estonia
5	Slovenia
4	Austria, Belgium, Hungary, Portugal
3	Finland, Greece
2	Denmark, France, Germany, Ireland, Poland, Slovakia, Spain, Sweden, United Kingdom
1	Luxembourg, Netherlands

Again, the breakdown favors countries from the northwest of Europe and disfavors many of the newer members. If these rates of turnover continue, the prospects for Italy and several of the post-Soviet countries could remain just as bleak as the chart suggested. Their lack of continuity will probably slow their economic growth, separating them even more from the leading groups of countries in the European Union. Differences that might have narrowed in recent years will begin to widen again. This finding might have been expected, because the reasons why these countries are in an economic hole now may well have something to do with their governments' past inability to take the long view.

When economic systems diverge, it can be very difficult to squeeze them back together. A cautionary example of this problem comes from the history of the United States. The Civil War, from 1861 to 1865, was about more than the moral question of slavery; the war was also a clash between two distinct economic systems. One of the motives for the Confederacy's secession was a desire to take charge of its own economic relations with the rest of the world, as parts of the European Union might also one day hope to do. Hundreds of thousands of people died before the Union was reaffirmed, and the complete integration of the nation's economic policy did not occur until the 1930s, even though the country was subject to a much stronger federal government than the one currently housed in Brussels.

The European Union may not need a civil war to emerge as a truly united economic entity with a single currency and perhaps even a harmonized fiscal policy, but it will need to exploit the complementarities between its component economies in a way that benefits all of them. If the wealthier countries with rosier futures care about holding the Union together, then they should help the poorer ones to get their budgetary houses in order, clean up their environments for doing business, and make investments for the future that will improve the potential for their economies to grow.

There is no time to lose. The death spiral caused by rising pension obligations and emigration of skilled workers may already be starting. We can't say for sure, because the European Union does not publish detailed figures on internal migration. Still, the writing is on the wall: if the Union does not act now to help the laggards keep up, then they will not be part of its march toward a brighter economic future.

PART · II

OBSTACLES

3

THE NEW COLONIALISM WILL LEAVE THE COLONIZERS AND THE COLONIZED WORSE OFF IN THE LONG TERM.

The deep factors that underpin an economy can determine the limits of its potential, but not every economy will reach that potential. An economy doesn't grow automatically; you can put all the underlying conditions in place, but you still need a constant supply of resources—including human resources—to make the great machine run. As an analogy, consider a sports car: you can build the fastest, sleekest car imaginable, but it still needs fuel. You can't just accumulate resources indiscriminately, either. A growing economy is engaged in a perpetual matching process: combining the right number of workers with the right amounts of raw materials, equipment, and financing to maximize workers' productivity, thus helping them achieve the highest possible wages and material living standards. To extend the analogy, you can't just fill your sports car with gasoline and expect it to work; you also need the right amounts of oil and fluids, as well as a competent driver.

Over long periods of time, a country's access to resources can change with little relationship to its cultural traditions, legal systems, or other deep factors. This means that even through shortages and surpluses an economy's potential to grow can remain the same: a sports car capable of 200 miles per hour with an empty fuel tank is still a sports car capable of 200 miles per hour. But those shortages and surpluses, and how a country deals with them, will determine whether and how quickly its potential is realized.

As the world's superpowers and up-and-coming economies try to realize their full economic potential, they will need a strong and steady flow of resources—sometimes more than they have access to in their own territory. Factories need minerals and metals. People need crops for food and clothing. Both need energy and water to keep running. Already, several countries that don't have all the resources they need—or want—are trying to enlarge their economic spheres of influence in parts of the developing world that are rich in commodities but poor in cash. A manic grab for resources, however, is likely to backfire in the long term.

FOR the European Union and the United States, the search for resources is pursued mainly by private companies and backed by international agreements on trade and investment. Yet it didn't always work that way—the United States and almost all early members of the European Union were once colonial powers. Governments and their franchisees, like the Abir Congo Company and the East India Company, managed the resources of foreign countries under the threat of force. Eventually, however, political, moral, and economic exigencies made their colonial holdings untenable.

As the traditional colonial powers gave up their last strongholds in Africa in the 1960s, a moment of unbridled optimism swept the developing world. Local people began to govern themselves, not just in Africa but in Latin America and East Asia as well. Many of their governments took a progressive path, investing their countries' labor and natural riches—the very resources the colonial powers had arrived to seize and control—in infrastructure, education, and public health. The first skyscrapers began to rise in African capitals. Primary schools were built in poor backwaters of Latin America where most people were illiterate. Land reform took place in East Asia, as tenant farmers transformed themselves into property owners for the first time.

These were heady times, and not always uniformly positive. In some countries, democratically elected leaders, like Ferdinand Marcos of the Philippines, used support from the West or from the Soviet Union to consolidate their power. The resulting dictatorships, often corrupt, would last for decades. In many other countries—Bolivia, Myanmar, and Uganda, to name a few—military men seized control, taking advantage of popular discontent and power vacuums when democratically elected governments became mired in scandal or political gridlock.

But in many cases, the independent governments of developing countries in the 1960s tried to modernize and share the wealth. Health, education, and infrastructure were their priorities. That redistributive bent looked to some outsiders like socialism, and indeed sometimes it was. Countries around the world saw socialism as an alternative to the capitalism—often more akin to rapacious mercantilism—of their former masters. Often, the Soviet Union was happy to help them pursue it, building a grain elevator in Afghanistan, a polytechnical institute in Guinea, a steel mill in India, a hospital in Indonesia, a stadium in Mali, and the famed Aswan High Dam in Egypt. As the eminent Sovietologist Marshall I. Goldman wrote in 1965, "The Russians have a knack for the spectacular."

Soviet aid, of course, was very much a consequence of Cold War priorities, and the West often reacted by trying to undermine the progress of these developing states. Inevitably, many politicians and generals saw the apparent embrace of socialism and its Soviet-provided trappings as a threat, and the hawks among them intervened to see that the most left-leaning of the new governments didn't stick around too long. Coups supported by the West toppled, among several others, Salvador Allende in Chile, Jacobo Arbenz Guzmán in Guatemala, Patrice Lumumba in the Democratic Republic of Congo, and Mohammad Mosaddeq in Iran. A few reasonably democratic governments survived, and a few more managed to unseat the colonizers' less savory successors. But in most countries, the promise of the postcolonial era quickly began to fade.

There were several reasons for this beyond the tribulations of the Cold War and internal politics. There were cross-border conflicts across Sub-Saharan Africa, Latin America, and the Middle East, sometimes supported by the Soviet Union and the West as proxy wars. Droughts, famines, and epidemics also hit poor countries around the world. Aid money was often mismanaged, wasted on useless projects, or spirited away by elites to overseas bank accounts; this was before the World Bank and others decided not to lend or give money to governments that were consistently corrupt.

Making matters worse, the borders of the world's biggest markets were not always open to the former colonies' exports. Worries about quality and sanitary standards, sometimes legitimate but often plainly protectionist, kept crops and textiles from poor countries out of the United States and Europe. This continues to be a problem today. The United States does give tariff-free access to products from many African and Latin American countries, as the European Union does with its former colonies in Africa, the Caribbean, and the Pacific. But since 1995, when the World Trade Organization was created, countries have filed more than ten thousand new rules on how plant and animal products must be prepared and tested for entry into their markets, including almost two thousand from the United States alone.

When developing countries did manage to export their products, they were often commodities with worldwide demand, like minerals, metals, and fuels. Yet corruption and oligarchic governments often meant this money was frittered away by top officials rather than put to work in the service of the populace. In Nigeria, for example, $300 billion in oil revenue simply disappeared over the course of three decades, according to the World Bank.

If the colonial period was one of supreme economic injustice, with palaces built in Western capitals thanks to the labor and resources of people thousands of miles away, then the period that came after old-style colonialism's final curtain was not much better. Some countries still managed to steady themselves and walk toward the future, though it wasn't necessarily the future they first imagined for themselves, nor were they walking as fast as they had planned.

Today, many developing countries find themselves in a delicate position. Their governments have control over some very valuable assets—minerals, metals, fuels, farmland—but they may not have the wherewithal to develop these assets into viable contributors to their economies. They have several options. First, they can do their best to turn the assets into earners, doing what they can with their own often meager human resources, technology, and finances: labor-intensive rather than highly automated agriculture and mining, small-scale oil and gas exploration and extraction rather than massive installations and offshore platforms. This is a slow road and potentially a difficult one, especially if citizens have to watch jealously as neighboring countries surge ahead. Second, they can accept help from international organizations like the World Bank, the United Nations Development Program, or the International Monetary Fund. But the money and expertise those organizations bring usually come with strings attached: a hand in writing new regulations, a say about how any resulting revenues might be used, and the burden of decades of debt.

A third option is to allow foreign operators in: branch offices, joint ventures, direct investments, privatizations, and even sales of national assets. This option is a tempting one, because governments can get money for resources up front without investing a dime of their own. For example, developing a natural gas field might cost $10 billion, but the gas, once extracted, could sell for as much as $50 billion in today's money over the course of several decades. A postcolonial government may not have the money or expertise to get at the gas, so it may try to engage some overseas help. The easiest way to do this is to have an auction for the rights to develop the gas field and sell the gas.

The winning bidder in the auction may be a single company, or a consortium of companies, or even a state agency from another country. But the winning bid won't necessarily be the $50 billion that the gas is worth over time; it will probably be much less, perhaps $20 billion or $30 billion. The bidder will be offering the government the proverbial bird in the hand, while being pretty sure that it will find two in the bush. Most politicians will be eager to accept.

Imagine the advantages for the politicians in question. If their government had decided to develop the gas field on its own, the revenues might not have started to flow into the treasury until years after they left office. By accepting an up-front payment in lieu of that promise of future revenue, they would be the ones with the power to cut taxes, spend money on social programs, create jobs, and invest in their people's future—and their successors would not. This government would have the once-in-a-lifetime chance to make a difference, to leave a lasting legacy—at least until some other government discovered more reserves of natural resources and started the whole process over again. And this discussion says nothing of corruption, an extra motivation for less-than-honest politicians to seek revenue sooner rather than later.

It's no surprise that this third option often wins. In recent times the governments of newly democratized countries like East Timor and Iraq have sold off the rights to develop billion-dollar oil fields within a few years of taking power. Western companies haven't been the only bidders and buyers; up-and-comers like Brazil's Petrobras and China's Sinopec have gotten in on the action, too. Oil isn't the only thing being sold, though. For example, a Chinese mining firm paid $27 billion for a controlling interest in a Namibian copper mine. In Angola, which also has oil and minerals, vast tracts of farmland are being sold off to foreign farmers and investors. The country's government has run a series of advertisements on international television news channels, with the slogan, "This is a place where everything can grow, with land as fertile as your dreams."

Buyers are only too happy to oblige. Responding to offers of land from Angola and Uganda, with deals reportedly in the works with Sudan and the Democratic Republic of Congo as well, the South African agriculture minister, Tina Joemat-Pettersson, said her government "encourages this type of expansion" and wants "to ensure that we broaden the base for commercial agriculture." Neighbors aren't the only ones interested: some countries will go much farther afield to find the resources they need. When Saudi Arabia's government was looking for new sources of food and water for its people a couple of years ago, it went to Pakistan and Sudan. "These countries have the land and the water," said a Bahraini agricultural official quoted at the time. "We have the money."

Food isn't the only reason the buyers are interested. They see purchases of land as a way to harness energy, too, through sources other than those buried under the ground. A consortium of German companies is leading a huge effort, estimated to cost well over half a trillion dollars, that will build solar energy fields in countries across North Africa. The electricity they generate will be routed to Europe, leaving the host countries to fend for themselves.

If it is the ready money that interests the sellers in these transactions, then it is the prospect of securing valuable resources for a growing future that interests the buyers. Yet their involvement in these developing countries, most of which sit a couple of steps lower on the skills ladder, brings some worrying possibilities. They are not just foreign businesses seeking to expand; they are state-run enterprises or government agencies that are extending their spheres of influence. And their involvement is only intensifying, with economic relationships turning into political relationships as well. Half a century after the death of European colonialism, a new type of colonialism is emerging. This time, instead of being taken over by force, countries are selling themselves.

IN principle, selling assets to an overseas buyer should be a harmless part of everyday life in the global economy. But these new relationships are often lopsided. China, Brazil, Saudi Arabia, and South Africa are in the top 35 in the world for gross domestic product. They have enormous buying power in the rest of the developing world, and their speedy growth, combined with the pools of cash in which their nascent markets are swimming, makes them hungrier to secure foreign acquisitions than their more developed counterparts. In these acquisitions, their governments play a starring role through control of agricultural projects, the national energy companies and, in China's case, the national mining companies as well.

So far, China and Saudi Arabia have led the way in acquisitions. According to news reports, China's state enterprises and agencies have spent at least a billion dollars to buy and develop mines, fuel deposits, and arable land (farms, paddies, or plantations) in the following countries: Angola, Australia, Canada, Chile, Congo, the Democratic Republic of Congo, Gabon, Guinea, Iran, Iraq, Kazakhstan, Laos, Mongolia, Myanmar, Peru, and the Philippines. Saudi Arabia's official investors have paid billions for oil in Malaysia and arable land in Egypt, Ethiopia, Indonesia, Sudan, and Turkey. Tens of thousands of square kilometers are changing hands, either permanently or on long-term leases.

Inevitably, the new wave of colonization, which is happening by piecework purchases rather than by wholesale occupation, will create economic and political arrangements that verge on the coercive. In 2006, a government minister in Zambia, Alice Simango, said that workers at a Chinese-owned coal mine were being treated like animals, and she closed the operation down for several days. More recently, a report covering ten countries by the African Labor Research Network found that Chinese employers were universally the worst in terms of pay and working conditions. Though it may be too early to assess the environmental impact of the new colonial arrangements, experts are warning that the colonizers' plans for land and water resources may not have the same goals as their hosts would choose. They might, for example, seek to maximize production for the short term rather than cautiously using fields, forests, and reservoirs to protect their long-term sustainability.

There is even a danger that citizens of colonized countries could lose the very land they are living on. Sometimes the colonizers offer compensation: China's Chinalco offered to pay $2,000 and provide new housing to families living in Morococha, a Chilean town that was slated to be destroyed as the company began mining the enormous mountain of copper ore on which it sat; a majority of the townspeople voted to accept the deal, and the rest were forced to go along. But in the poorest countries, where millions of people still live as subsistence farmers, growing barely enough food to feed their families, the issue of land rights is particularly difficult.

Consider the situation of farming families in the rural north of Cambodia, who have been farming the same land the same way for generations. If you ask them and their neighbors, there is no doubt about which pieces of land belong to whom.

Yet most of them don't have a piece of paper that states their ownership of the land; they don't have any legal title that would hold up in court, and many of them are illiterate anyway. As a result, colonizers can move in, buying large swaths of land directly from the government, perhaps with a carefully placed bribe here or there to move the process along. For example, Cambodia has become one of the targets of government agencies in South Korea that are also buying up land in Africa, Russia, and South America. Sometimes the Cambodian farmers don't even find out about the sale until the colonizers, or sometimes the police or army who are supposed to protect them, arrive to kick them off their land. A program led by the World Bank issued more than a million land titles to poor people in Cambodia over several years, but the Cambodian government shut down the program in 2009 just as hundreds of poor families were being evicted from their homes because of the expansion of urban areas.

As the colonizers build up their holdings in a country, they begin to exert a powerful influence that goes beyond simply smoothing over the bureaucracy with bribes. South Africa, a potential colonizer with an economic reach stretching midway up the continent, is itself being colonized by China. At the end of 2008, there were a thousand Chinese firms registered to do business in South Africa, and they had committed a total of $50 billion in capital investments. One of those investments was a Chinese bank's purchase of 20 percent of Standard Bank, South Africa's biggest lender. In general, a stake that size is big enough to control a public company. And in 2009, China overtook the United States as the biggest destination for South African exports, having increased its trade with the country tenfold in ten years—an appropriate position for a dominant colonial power.

China's influence in Pretoria came to the fore when South Africa denied the Dalai Lama a visa to attend an antixenophobia conference in Johannesburg. South African officials publicly

denied that China had forced the decision. Speaking anonymously to the South African newspaper *Business Day*, however,
one of them let the cat out of the bag: the government had
been worried that the visit would upset its Chinese patrons.
"We would not do anything to upset the relationship we have
with China," the official said. But by allowing a foreign country to take over control of its borders, even just for one case,
South Africa had surrendered part of its sovereignty.

The fact that state agencies in China, Saudi Arabia, South
Korea, and other countries are at the heart of deals for territory
is crucial in making these relationships colonial rather than
simply commercial. If a multinational company had bought
up all the territory mentioned above, it might try to affect
policies that involved its business by influencing local governments, but it might not take the trouble to affect how the
countries in question were aligned in matters of international
politics. Even if it had wanted to, what threats could it make?
To pull out of investments in the countries? China, with its
many roles as investor, exporter, arms dealer, regional superpower, and permanent member of the United Nations Security Council, can exert much more influence than any single
company.

THE scope of the buying by the new colonizers is breathtaking.
China is losing about 8,000 square kilometers of arable land
each year to desertification, and more to pollution. To replace
that land and keep up with rising demand, it might have to buy
much more territory in foreign countries. Pretty soon, those
holdings will add up. At a rate of, say, about 25,000 square kilometers a year, China will buy territory equal in size to the
United Kingdom every decade.

This doesn't mean that China, Saudi Arabia, and other
potential colonizers will buy up whole countries. But in a very
short period of time, they could start to exert a powerful

influence in the economies where they put down roots. For example, take China's billion-dollar investment in palm oil plantations in the Democratic Republic of Congo. That country's gross domestic product is worth less than $12 billion a year, so the investment is massive by its standards. The Democratic Republic of Congo also cultivates less than 5 percent of its potentially arable land, according to the U.S. Central Intelligence Agency's publicly available statistics, so there is a huge amount of room for expansion. For China, the investment is tiny; its annual output is almost four hundred times larger than that of the Democratic Republic of Congo. With more blockbuster purchases, it could farm enough so that the gross domestic product of its territory might far exceed that of the rest of the country. Chinese Congo would be a bigger mark on the economic map than the country that was its notional home.

The Congolese people and their government may not complain about this situation as long as they are handsomely compensated. Yet dealing with such an enormous inflow of money is not always easy. Imagine if helicopters suddenly dropped a billion dollars in cash all around the Democratic Republic of Congo—what would happen? In the short term, the amount of stuff available for Congolese people to buy would be the same; you can't dramatically increase the output of the economy overnight, nor can you import vast amounts of merchandise from one day to another. As a result, a huge amount of new money will be chasing roughly the same quantity of goods and services in the economy. Only one thing can happen: prices will rise.

Later, the economy might overheat as it struggles to catch up with the artificial increase in demand. It is for this reason that Norway, which has enormous petroleum reserves, invests all the revenue from selling oil outside of Norway. In the short term, the economy cannot always absorb such an inflow of money. A wise government might save the money, investing in projects to improve economic growth and human development as they become available.

Besides money for their territory, what do colonized countries receive in return under these new arrangements? In the old days, they were exploited, sometimes mercilessly, with their people brutalized and kept in servitude. They were excluded from education, and the economic plan for the colonized territory was intended only to benefit the colonizers. The new colonizers may not enslave the people where they take over territory, but they may not feel much obligation to help the colonized people to improve their living standards. So far, China and Saudi Arabia have been content to pay their money up front and then focus on their own economic endeavors.

The responsibility to ensure that local people benefit in some way from the relationship falls squarely on the shoulders of the colonized country's government. This might be fine if the colonizers actually took pains to ensure that they only invested in countries with democratic governments that sought to help their people. But China, Saudi Arabia, and the other colonizers don't seem to make much of a distinction. Just weeks after the government of Guinea killed 157 pro-democracy demonstrators in its capital, Conakry, in September 2009, a Chinese mining firm signed a $7 billion deal to extract the country's metals and gemstones. What would happen to that money? Transparency International ranked Guinea as the 168th (tied) least corrupt country out of 180 in 2009, and the World Bank's *Governance Matters* report placed it among the worst in the world for government effectiveness, political stability, and the rule of law in 2008. With an ineffective, corrupt government in charge—and perhaps not for very long, given the country's volatile recent history—the fate of the money was anyone's guess.

DESPITE these concerns, some experts on development, notably Jeffrey Sachs of Columbia University, argue that new colonial investments do more good than harm. Indeed, history suggests that there are some long-term positive effects for the colonized countries, though it depends who colonizes them. When the British administered countries and territories, they usually installed a legal system similar to their own, which was based on the common law tradition that dates back to the Magna Carta. This tradition emphasized the rights of the individual and allowed governing principles to evolve through case law. By contrast, French and German colonizers adhered to their own legal traditions, which descended from the civil law system whose precedents included Roman law and the Napoleonic Code. These systems were more committed to upholding abstract ideas, which could then be interpreted by judges and rulers as they saw fit.

In the postcolonial period, countries with common law systems provided greater protection for investors and were less likely to be subverted by powerful or corrupt individuals for their personal gain. As a result, financial systems developed more broadly, which in turn provided the backbone for capital markets and economic growth. Being colonized was not necessarily a boon in itself, but in the case of the former British colonies, it at least left one useful inheritance.

Yet this happy (or at least not all bad) example is unlikely to be repeated by the new wave of colonizers. For starters, the countries they are colonizing have already been colonized once, and their legal systems are already firmly in place. It's unlikely that the colonizers will be allowed to wipe the slate clean and install their own institutions. Even if they could, their institutions may not be so favorable to economic development. The Chinese legal system is heavily bureaucratic, is not independent from the authoritarian government, and grants few rights to defendants. The legal systems of the Gulf nations generally have their basis in a combination of tribal and Islamic law, neither of which is particularly favorable to entrepreneurship or the development of financial markets. For example, Islamic law complicates debt-based financing (because of a religious prohibition on charging interest) and does not recognize the concept of a corporation.

These findings fit neatly into a popular strain of thought that now runs through the literature of academic economics. At its core is the idea that developing countries can benefit from importing economic institutions like free markets, strong property rights, and investor protections from wealthy countries. To date, some developing countries have done this by allowing economic laboratories to function on their territory, testing policies that might someday apply more broadly, as in India's special economic zones or in Hong Kong, which has been a special administrative region of China since 1997. Others have allowed foreign practices to creep into their business climates through joint ventures with companies from wealthy countries.

Indeed, even the starkest form of colonization—taking control of land in another country through purchase or other means—can be helpful in the right context. An economist could argue, for example, that Haiti's agriculture, which is still based on the smallholdings that arose out of the Haitian revolution in the early nineteenth century, would benefit from a takeover; a foreign power might bundle up those tiny parcels into huge farms that could be harvested with modern equipment, freeing up labor for more capital-intensive, higher-value occupations. In this fashion, colonization would help people in developing countries take the first step up the skills ladder, escaping from subsistence agriculture on a family plot.

Of course, many of those people might prefer to hold on to their land. And again, there is always the danger that foreign companies and even foreign governments will indulge in behavior that is not tolerated in their home countries, exploiting local resources without regard for long-term economic effects. They are, after all, essentially involved in a for-profit enterprise, just as the German East Africa Company and the Dutch and British East India Companies were in their day.

WHERE the new colonization does occur, many of its positive and negative effects will naturally be visible to the citizens of the colonized countries. How they react will determine the future of the colonial relationships and, to some degree, all the countries involved.

Most obvious to the colonized will be the enormous sales of their countries' resources. So far, no country has launched a program specifically linking the sale of land or natural resources to improvements in its people's living standards; no government has said, "We sold ten thousand hectares of our land to Saudi Arabia, and we will use all the money we received to construct one hundred new hospitals across the country." Naturally, you would expect countries with better run, less corrupt, and more accountable governments to use the money more wisely, just as they already use their existing funds. The governments of those countries—democracies like Chile and Canada, for example—already enjoy more of their people's confidence than those of, say, Gabon and Myanmar, which are ruled, respectively, by the son of a former president who won a heavily disputed election after his father's death and by a military junta.

When the sales of natural assets are not accompanied by improvements in basic living standards, citizens do tend to react negatively; we have already seen ample evidence of this phenomenon in corporate deals that were not strictly colonialist. For instance, the ongoing insurgency in the Niger Delta is largely a result of the failure of the Nigerian government and its corporate partners to share their profits from nearby oil ventures with the local tribes. In 2006 in East Timor, the government faced riots when money gained from selling the rights to offshore oil exploration did not turn immediately into jobs for the country's unemployed, who made up one-fifth of the workforce at that time. The reasons why wealth did not translate into well-being were different— neglect and corruption in Nigeria, and worries that the economy could not suddenly absorb billions of dollars in East Timor—but the results were the same.

Neither Nigeria nor East Timor uses as much oil as it produces, so shortages aren't the problem. But imagine what would happen if these countries were actually exporting things their people needed and used every day, like food. How will the Sudanese react, for example, when they see their own people starve while Saudi companies harvest crops on Sudanese land, solely for export back to Saudi Arabia?

The world got a peek at the answer in early 2008, when high food prices led to protests and riots in countries in Africa, the Americas, and Asia. Under pressure from citizens, several countries halted exports of crops altogether in an effort to ensure that their own people would be able to eat, at least in the short term. Brazil, Cambodia, and India were among those that stopped shipments of rice, predictably eliciting protests from import-dependent countries like Saudi Arabia.

A temporary hold on exports may not be an available solution for newly colonized countries, however. That option doesn't exist when a country's government doesn't actually control its own exports. Most of the agreements being signed by the new colonizers grant long-term or permanent rights to the output from farms, mines, or fuel deposits. Depending on the colonized countries' economic situations, reneging on those agreements could be disastrous, perhaps even more disastrous than letting some of their own people go without food.

Yet reneging is exactly what some countries probably will do. Politicians usually put their own power above any other consideration, so annoying a foreign power might be preferable to risking electoral defeat or a coup. Indeed, the governments of Hugo Chávez in Venezuela and Evo Morales in Bolivia have scored political points with their citizens by renationalizing resources and industries dominated by foreign companies, which were forced to accept derisory payoffs or simply kicked out of the country. The pressure to engage in this behavior will be strongest in countries that hover close to the line of self-sufficiency, but also in those that fail to diversify their economies into industries other than the ones dominated by the colonizing powers. It will also happen if the assets turn out to be much more valuable than originally anticipated. Copper, a material so far unmatched for its combination of electric conductivity, malleability, and low price, is in limited supply. China is rapidly acquiring gigantic copper mines around the world. If the price of copper were to spike, locals who sold their mines to China might look back covetously upon those assets. When prices rise, commodities don't have to be edible to be desirable.

WHAT happens when the colonies rebel? When the foreign oil, gas, steel, and cement companies were renationalized in South America, the governments in their home countries offered a few mild words of protest—and that was all. The governments of China, Saudi Arabia, and other colonizers may not knuckle under quite so easily, but their options for enforcing economic priorities are hardly attractive. Would Saudi Arabia send warships and troops to protect its farms and rice paddies in Indonesia? Would it simply bulk up security on its farms to repel local invaders, delineating its territory even more strongly as a colony? Or would it use its economic power as an oil dealer and importer to force the Indonesians to back down? And if the Indonesian government backs down, will its people revolt? There can't be many things more galling than going hungry while your government allows a foreign power to export food from what was once your land. To fill the bellies of their people without angering their colonial masters, the governments of colonized countries might resort to war and conquest of their neighbors.

These problems will be nothing new to students of colonial history. The colonial powers gave their territories independence not just because it was the right thing to do, but because they decided that buying commodities on the open market might be easier than managing a foreign land thousands of miles away, especially when it was becoming harder to stop arms from flowing into that land. And conflict is not the only factor that might make colonizers think twice. Raw materials may not be as copious or easy to extract as the colonizers had hoped. Technological changes can make some fuels and metals less important to the global economy, and thus less valuable. People's tastes can change, too, and the assets bought today may not be as desirable tomorrow. The uncertainty that the colonized swap with the colonizers for ready cash is still there, and it creates risks for the colonizers just as it does for the colonized.

These risks don't seem to have dampened the colonizers' enthusiasm, however. They are just as worried about their political fortunes as the governments that sell them land. If the colonizers fail to provide enough food for their people or enough raw materials to keep their factories running, they could be expelled from their positions of power—perhaps forcibly, in the case of governments that weren't democratically elected, like China's and Saudi Arabia's. After all, those two governments are already fighting outbreaks of unrest on a regular basis: rioting migrant workers and displaced landowners in China, and Islamic terrorism and secessionists in Saudi Arabia. Just as for the colonized, maintaining stability in the short term is the first priority; the consequences in the future may end up being someone else's problem.

Nevertheless, there are ways of protecting a colonial invest-ment in the long term. The most obvious is to safeguard stabil-ity in the colonized country. So far, there is little evidence that the colonizers are trying to ensure that their new influence leads to better living standards for colonized people, either through their own efforts or in partnership with local govern-ments. Yet this kind of cooperation can take many forms, such as training local people to take higher-skilled jobs in colonized territories, paying for public health and education programs in colonized communities, distributing a share of export revenue directly to local people and municipal leaders, or signing agree-ments with governments to pay for colonial territory over a long period of time to ensure there is capacity to use the money productively.

Many years ago, a model in these respects was the Soviet Union and its overseas industrial projects. As Marshall Gold-man wrote in 1965, "The Soviets also take pride in their train-ing of native technicians. Some are sent to the Soviet Union and others are trained on the job. Immense patience is required; but the Russians normally feel that training is more important than speed." Just recently, China has begun to work toward a more cooperative and less exploitative relationship with its colonial hosts. A three-year program will attempt to build scientific and technological capacity in forty-nine African countries—almost the entire continent—through links between universities and vocational schools.

For the colonizing powers, it will be essential to consider such programs now, while the colonial wave is in its infancy. If they do not create economic and social frameworks for stabil-ity now, the future may offer only one option for stemming conflict in their colonies: the use of force.

ON the other side of the coin, countries that are candidates for colonization will want to think about how to protect themselves from being exploited. They can simply say no, as Angola, Australia, and Libya have done by refusing new deals with the Chinese. They can set down laws to protect the rights of their citizens, from environmental regulations to workplace safety rules. They can also try to make sure that their citizens share in the bonanza of foreign investment through minimum wages or taxes on the new ventures. But all of these measures are likely to make potential investors think twice about putting their money into a country; they'd probably rather find another place with fewer restrictions, where they can keep more of their profits for themselves. Even the most well-intentioned government will have to consider the trade-off: more funds flowing in versus more risks for its people.

At the very least, countries facing colonization can ensure that their citizens maintain the rights to the property they already own, as the World Bank and its partners tried to do in Cambodia. Even if the rights of colonized peoples can be protected, however, new spheres of influence will still arise. China and Saudi Arabia don't have thousands of overseas security forces now, but they might decide to change that situation if they see the need to defend their new territories. Neither country is known for its defense of human rights and democracy. In fact, they are actively cultivating relationships with many governments that have been ostracized by the global community because of violations of civil rights. The Chinese in particular, like the Soviets before them, rush to fill the void when countries in the West cut off relations with pariah states like Iran, Myanmar, and Sudan.

It is for this very reason that many colonial relationships will fail. Twenty-two countries were listed above as having done deals with China and Saudi Arabia. In the World Bank's *Governance Matters* ranking of 212 countries and territories for control of corruption—defined as "public power being exercised for private gain" and " 'capture' of the state by elites and private interests"—all but five ranked in the bottom half. Will these countries' governments truly use revenue from the sale of natural assets to help their people? Not likely. Their people will be the losers in these neocolonial arrangements, and, when they get sufficiently fed up to revolt, the colonizers will lose as well. Having counted on their colonies to produce the commodities they needed, the colonizers will find themselves facing shortages and an equally angry populace at home. At that point, the results of colonialism will be much the same as they were a century ago, and more: economic exploitation, retardation of development, local instability, and, at some point in the future, a glib and perhaps grudging good-bye.

4

CHANGING IMMIGRATION POLICIES IN RICH COUNTRIES WILL WORSEN THE BRAIN DRAIN FROM POOR COUNTRIES, EVEN AS THEY GET RICHER.

An economy uses only two types of resources as it grows: natural resources and human resources. Everything an economy produces is made by combining the raw materials found in nature with the ideas and labor humans provide. And just as growing economies can face shortages of natural resources, so can they face shortages of human resources; each is a formidable obstacle to growth.

Also, as with natural resources, there are only two ways to replenish human resources: grow them on your own territory or import them. This is where the similarities end. Many natural resources can be grown in a short period of time, but making human resources from scratch takes decades. Importing them is a much faster solution.

In modern economic history, labor has been imported with its consent and against its will. But at no time has immigration been as great a success as when labor *wanted* to move. This stands to reason, since the opportunities for labor are greatest when it is most needed; wages rise when employers are desperate to attract new workers. Yet labor can't move as freely around the world as oil, gold, or wheat.

Immigration is a very controversial topic, for reasons that

have become clear in countless political debates around the world. The stereotypical pros of immigration are that new arrivals almost always come to work, they enrich local cultures, and they add to the tax base. The stereotypical cons of immigration are that new arrivals take jobs away from native-born people, they fail to adapt to local customs, and they use up public services. Then there is the thorny issue of illegal immigration, which is usually seen as a political evil but, in reality, is frequently an economic necessity.

Because of the political sensitivity of immigration, flows of labor have lagged far behind flows of money and merchandise during the current wave of economic globalization. In the past one hundred and fifty years in the United States, the number of people granted permanent residency has fluctuated dramatically from year to year, from a low of 23,068 in 1933 to an all-time high of 1,826,595 in 1991. The immediate causes of the changes have almost always been political, with social and economic motivations in the background. Immigration was a tougher sell during the Great Depression when so many Americans were unemployed; the low in 1933 was less than one-tenth the total of permanent residencies granted in 1930. Yet the quota system used to contain immigration in the 1930s had actually been instituted because of a law passed in 1924, a result of growing isolationist sentiment. The peak in 1991 came as a result of a political deal, too: a law passed in 1986 had offered amnesty and a path to legal residence to millions of illegal workers, but at the same time it criminalized the hiring of illegal immigrants and tightened other controls on immigrant workers. As a result, the number of permanent residencies granted on an annual basis almost tripled between 1988 and 1991.

Other countries have also suffered the political slings and arrows of the immigration debate. In the European Union, immigration is an internal as well as external issue. The addition of ten new members, mostly former Soviet satellites, in

2004 caused a massive churning of the Union's population, with hundreds of thousands of people moving west, at least temporarily, in an effort to find better jobs and living standards. In France, this phenomenon led to widespread talk of the "Polish plumber," a stereotypical figure who came to embody the potential for immigrants to take professional jobs that would otherwise have gone to French people.

In addition to dealing with internal migration, the southernmost countries in Europe are also targets for immigrants from North Africa and the Middle East, as well as nearby countries that have not yet joined the Union, like Albania and Moldova. In Italy and Spain, immigration is as divisive an issue as it is in the United States, with governments from both right and left seeking greater control of their countries' borders. And all across the Union there is a continuous flow of migrants, most of them illegal, from the more troubled parts of the Middle East and Central Asia; many do not stop going west until they reach the United Kingdom. Some will be granted asylum, but many will stay on illegally or be sent back to their countries of origin.

Countries do not have to be rich to worry about immigration. For example, tens and perhaps hundreds of thousands of refugees from the conflicts in Sudan have fled to Chad, putting even more stress on a country that was already poorer than its war-torn neighbor. Indeed, no country of any significant size has unfiltered, unlimited, legal immigration. At the very least, there are always some criteria to meet in order to enter.

Yet despite the politicization of the immigration issue, economic realities always have their say. In recent years, admissions of temporary workers in the United States have shot up from about 1.2 million in 1999 to almost 2 million in 2008. The number of illegal immigrants has been estimated at close to 12 million, a number built up from arrivals that date back to the 1980s. If American industries need foreign workers, they will find them either legally or illegally.

In addition, outsourcing and offshoring have provided new ways to tap overseas labor without letting it cross the border. The use of these practices has only intensified as developing countries become integrated into the global trading system, becoming ever more sophisticated in their commercial relations with wealthier economies. Anything, it seems, is preferable to actual immigration because of the potential for political consequences. But soon, all of this will change.

IMMIGRATION policies will change because they have to, because of what will be happening in countries both rich and poor. Demographically and economically, both groups of countries will be undergoing a transformation that will simply be incompatible with their current immigration policies.

In several of the biggest rich countries, the demand for immigrant labor is going to rise over the next few decades. Until better robots are developed, there will always be a certain number of low-paying jobs that can only be done by people. Those jobs are usually site-specific; in other words, you can't prune the trees in someone's garden via the Internet from your home office, nor can you offshore that work to someone in India. The gardener has to be there, just like the nanny, the maid, and the home health aide. In some of these cases, it might be possible to develop a high-technology alternative to a human worker, but doing so isn't worthwhile; the human workers may actually cost less than the mechanical option.

As a rule, these jobs become more numerous when a country's population gets richer. People move into bigger houses, so they have more gardens. They work at jobs where the value of their time is greater, so they decide to hire a nanny instead of staying home and taking care of their young children themselves. They also have more money to spend on other services where the people who provide the labor aren't usually paid much: manicures, personal training sessions, grocery delivery, and so on.

These people are getting richer because the skill levels in their country are rising; the workforce is moving up the technological ladder, producing goods and services whose value is rising higher and higher. For exactly that reason, these people are much less likely to accept a job as a gardener or a nanny. In their country, not only is the demand for people to do these low-paying jobs increasing, the supply of people willing to do them is falling at the same time.

This shortage will grow as long as the skill level of the native-born population keeps rising, simply because it is either impossible or not economical to automate all of these low-skilled jobs. Immigrants from poorer countries whose workers have skills that are less highly prized in the global labor market are the natural choice to fill the gap. And from an economic perspective, there's nothing wrong with having them do exactly that; the immigrants free up the higher-skilled people to do their highly productive jobs and enjoy the fruits of their labor.

Added to this economic pressure will be demographic pressure. Rich countries tend to have lower fertility rates than do poor countries, and quite a few rich countries now have shrinking populations. Germany, Italy, and Japan all lost population in 2009. Looking into the next several decades, they face the prospect that this shrinkage will start to drag down their economies, too. That doesn't necessarily mean their people will have lower living standards—after all, there will be fewer of them slicing up the economic pie—but it will mean a drop in their power on global markets and a reduction of their clout in global politics. For countries with proud heritages as international heavyweights, that prospect may be unacceptable. They will need more people, and there are only two choices: have more babies or let in more immigrants.

The demographic pressure also has other, more immediate, consequences. In the next few decades, the population of working age will not grow or will grow only negligibly in most of the world's major wealthy economies. This may not sound so dire, but imagine a situation where a new industry arises, or an existing industry suddenly starts to grow much more quickly than before—say, for example, the alternative energy industry. To underpin that growth, the industry needs an influx of skilled labor. If the overall size of the workforce is not changing, the industry will have to steal that labor from other industries. On balance, this shift of labor would benefit the economy. Yet the other industries haven't necessarily become less productive; the best thing for the economy would be to keep them at their current size while the alternative energy industry continues to grow. To accomplish this outcome, however, the economy will need more skilled workers. Again, there are only two ways to get them: wait for a new group of workers to achieve the high skill levels required or allow immigrants to come in right away and bolster the workforce.

Because the first solution implies a delay, it also implies that some productive potential will be lost while the economy waits for the new generation of skilled workers to appear. Countries that have become wealthy quickly have been especially conscious of this possibility. In several of the oil-rich nations of the Middle East, migrant workers handily outnumber the native-born population. While the locals collect shares of the oil and gas revenue they consider their patrimony, the migrants do the jobs that allow the country to function and grow—not just blue-collar jobs like construction and housecleaning, which typically go to South and Southeast Asians, but also white-collar jobs like corporate management and consulting, which are dominated by Europeans.

This loss of productive potential because of a shortage of appropriately skilled workers will be especially deep if governments of rich countries continue to increase their investments in basic scientific research, as they are doing now. In line with mainstream economists' best thinking, the United States ramped up funding for research in response to the global economic crisis of 2008. The money provides an immediate stimulus, because much of it is spent on high-tech equipment manufactured in wealthy countries, as well as on researchers' wages. But by spurring innovation, it also greatly enhances these economies' potential to grow in the future. That higher potential makes the cost of diverting scarce labor to low-skilled jobs even greater.

This would not be the only cost of deciding against immigration, however. Many of the same governments of wealthy countries, including the United States, now carry enormous debts and other future obligations. These liabilities have three recent sources: deficits incurred because of low tax revenue during the global downturn, debts created by unprecedented stimulus spending, and promises of pensions and medical benefits to citizens who have yet to retire.

The promises will be especially difficult to fulfill because most wealthy countries have pay-as-you-go social security systems. In a pay-as-you-go system, taxes collected today are used to pay today's retirement benefits; today's workers pay for today's retirees, and today's workers will have their benefits paid by tomorrow's workers. This kind of system generally works fine as long as each generation of workers is larger or earns more than the previous generation. But in many of these countries, the coming cohorts of retiring workers will be the largest in history. The taxpayers who will finance their benefits will come from smaller cohorts; the burden each of them will have to bear will be bigger than the burdens borne by any previous generations.

The gap between the benefits already promised to retirees and the tax revenue being collected from current workers is potentially enormous. It is well known that the Social Security system in the United States faces insolvency within a couple of decades, but in 2005 the nation was spending only 6 percent of its gross domestic product on public pensions. By contrast, Italy, Austria, France, Greece, Poland, Germany, and Portugal were already spending at least 10 percent, with Italy topping out at 14 percent. Benefits look likely to fall, yet cutting them could be politically impossible: current retirees will protest as their income declines, and current workers will rebel if offered benefits inferior to the ones they financed for the older generation.

Those current workers will also be responsible for paying the enormous debts incurred in the past few years as governments around the world tried to rescue the financial system and their individual economies from crisis through emergency spending. Once more, there will be two choices: renege on the promises made to creditors and future retirees, or allow immigrants to shoulder part of the burden by joining the tax base.

CLEARLY, there is a greater role for immigration in the future economic policy of many countries, especially wealthy ones. As governments begin to change course, two questions will naturally arise: what kind of people should we let in, and how many? Because this change of course will have primarily economic motivations, it's likely that the answers to those questions will be economically motivated as well. Once countries have let in enough people to fill low-wage positions, they will want to shift all the way to the other end of the spectrum, cherry-picking the "best" immigrants: the most inventive, the most educated, the highest earners, the easiest to integrate.

This goal will lead to some fascinating dynamics. If every government is trying to attract the best migrants, we will see the greatest international beauty contest in history. Countries around the globe will struggle to offer the biggest welcome to the millions of doctors, scientists, engineers, inventors, and entrepreneurs who might be looking for a new home. Two factors will enter immigrants' calculations as they judge the contest: how easy it is to get into their new country and what sort of life they will have once they arrive.

Based on these factors, we can already see some potential winners and losers lining up on the stage. First, economic immigrants generally find wealthier countries more attractive, especially when they have skills with high value in the labor market. The lion's share of professional, educated migrants will be looking for a home where the resources are available to ply their trades; it's much easier to be an organic chemist in Canada, where laboratory space is relatively plentiful, than in Cambodia. This dynamic will not only benefit the wealthiest countries but also large countries that are growing quickly, like Brazil and China. Undoubtedly, thousands of Brazilians and Chinese who previously emigrated to more advanced economies will come back in an attempt to harness the rapid growth of their home countries for their personal enrichment. Countries that invest heavily in the fields in which they hope to attract immigrants will benefit as well. For example, South Korea's government science foundation was spending more money on research, proportional to the country's population, than the U.S. National Science Foundation did until the budget increases of Barack Obama's administration. (And incidentally, South Korea will need all the help it can give itself; as of 2009, its net migration rate was negative; that is, more people were leaving the country than settling there.)

Second, there is an enormous advantage in being an English-speaking country. English is already the international language of science, medicine, and technology; most of the professionals a government would want to attract already speak the language at some level, and it is the most commonly taught second language in the world. To be sure, the second generation in most immigrant families will pick up the local language, whatever it is, without any trouble. Attracting the first generation is the key to the whole process, however. Score one for the United Kingdom and its former colonies around the world.

How countries select their migrants will also play a fundamental role in their economic fates. In 2002, the United Kingdom launched a new initiative called the Highly Skilled Migrant Program as an adjunct to its existing immigration policy. Under the program, potential immigrants were graded on a points system based on their education, earning history, age, level of English proficiency, and other factors. High scorers would be granted a work permit and a path to citizenship, even if they had no job in hand or even any contacts in the United Kingdom. In 2003, a new section was added to the program to select the most gifted younger migrants. And in 2008, the program became the first tier of the country's mainstream immigration policy. The points calculator was available online, and potential applicants who scored enough points to be approved—a Ph.D. alone was worth two-thirds of the necessary total—were told, "If you wish to immigrate to the UK now, it is almost certain that you can pass the points system," and were given an e-mail address and phone number for an immigration advisor. The path to citizenship takes just six years.

Other countries, including Australia, Canada, and New Zealand, have points systems as well. But in countries like the United States, even the most highly skilled migrants may still have a hard time gaining a work or residency permit. Unlike in the United Kingdom, there is an annual quota for all employment-related applications for permanent residency, which can be as low as 140,000 per year. That total includes everyone from "priority workers"—internationally known executives, researchers, and the like—to unskilled workers needed by basic industries. There are programs for temporary workers, too, but these require potential immigrants to have a job offer waiting. In addition, they generally have limiting quotas, and they don't run on a points system.

The lack of an unlimited, transparent points system isn't the only thing that might steer talented migrants away from countries like the United States and toward countries like the United Kingdom. The welcome they can expect to receive will make a difference, too. This factor could be a problem for countries like Switzerland, whose population is aging incredibly quickly. Right now, the Swiss population aged forty to fifty— people who will retire in a decade or two—is almost twice as large as the population aged ten or younger. Yet immigration in Switzerland is extremely difficult; you have to live there for twelve years, pass a battery of cultural and linguistic tests, and then be approved by a vote of your neighbors.

Japan, whose population is actually shrinking and may fall by as much as a quarter by 2050, is also loath to admit the immigrants it will imminently need. In the past, Japan rarely welcomed immigrants with open arms. Foreign-born people constitute only 1.6 percent of Japan's population, in contrast to about 12 percent in the United States. A few years ago, a United Nations envoy found that Japanese attitudes toward foreigners manifested themselves in "profound discrimination of a cultural and historical nature" and called the immigration bureau's anonymous tip line for illegal immigration cases "an incitement to racism, racial discrimination and xenophobia."

If Japan does not change this situation, the results for its economy could be dramatic. The Census Bureau projects that the population of the United States will grow by more than 40 percent by 2050. If the productivity of workers grows at roughly the same rate in the two countries, then Japan's output could go from being about one-third the size of the United States's to less than one-fifth. In fact, the difference is likely to be even greater; the productivity of workers in the United States has been growing more quickly since the 1990s, and there is little evidence to suggest that trend will change.

Even if Japan can maintain its citizens' standards of living in the midst of these changes, the overall size of its economy will still shrink relative to other countries. That will have very real effects: a smaller voice in organizations like the International Monetary Fund and the World Bank, less interest from potential trading partners seeking new markets for exports, and the risk of being left in China's shadow as a regional player.

Now, the Japanese people may indeed prefer to recede to the margins of the economic and geopolitical stages rather than allow more immigrants into their country. That is their decision. But because Japan's society is aging, the money to pay for pensions already promised to retiring workers simply will not appear unless something transformative occurs—for example, if the country were to experience an increase in productivity akin to the one that followed World War II, when it catapulted itself from destitution to the top flight of the world's economies. Or Japan could try to boost the percentage of potential workers who participate in the labor force; at the time of this writing, only 60 percent of the working-age population was either seeking or already in full-time employment. To do that, however, might require a cultural change even more abrupt than giving immigrants a warm welcome. Even if these changes do occur, it will be over the course of decades. In the meantime, retirement benefits will have to be cut, and Japan's elderly—as well as the younger people who support them—will be permanently poorer.

Japan is an extreme case, but it shows the direction in which many wealthy countries are heading. In the United States, too, the stagnation of the labor force will favor the loosening of immigration quotas, even as worries about terrorism have made immigration policies more restrictive, not less. Yet if those wealthy countries in a struggle to save their own economies and budget balances are successful in attracting the world's best and brightest, it will not necessarily be good news for the entire world. The resulting situation in poor countries could be downright dire.

IN the past half-century or so, economists' thinking about how poor countries grow has gone through several major changes. At first, the mainstream embraced the idea that huge infrastructural projects and top-down management would spur investment and economic growth. Then, economists came up with a series of prescriptions for specific policies—on interest rates and the money supply, taxes and spending, and trade policy and exchange rates—that they believed would help any country to emerge from poverty. Later on, about a decade ago, public health and then education became the essential ingredients for escaping a life of bare subsistence; nothing could change until these basic necessities were in place, and further changes needed to be tailored to each region, each country, and even each village. And now, the thinking is changing again: micro-capitalism, achieved by creating strong property rights, enriching credit markets, and seeding entre-preneurship, is the way forward. The idea is that if talented locals stay in their own countries, they will be able to take responsibility for the other problems—public health, educa-tion, infrastructure, and industrial development—and solve them on their own, rather than depending solely on foreign aid. Creating a welcoming environment for entrepreneurs will also help to bring back expatriates who have picked up valu-able knowledge, skills, and connections abroad.

Of course, the true path is likely to have something in com-mon with all of these ideas, but one thing is certain: to make sure that economic growth sticks, poor countries need to make sure they hold on to their most capable citizens. The alterna-tive is another form of colonialism: foreigners in all the impor-tant posts in the economy, the locals barely invested in their own future.

Globalization has already resulted in a global brain drain, despite the fact that not all countries welcome talented immigrants with open arms. A report released by the Arab League in 2009 found that roughly 100,000 scientists, doctors, and engineers were leaving countries in the Middle East and North Africa every year, with the bulk of the scientists and doctors never returning. Another study suggested that vast numbers of developing countries' doctors were working abroad, including 41 percent from Jamaica, 35 percent from Haiti, 30 percent from Ghana, 27 percent from Sri Lanka, and 18 percent from South Africa. The brain drain has even worried some wealthy countries; the government of New Zealand, for instance, launched a program in 2006 to try to lure its huge expatriate population back home.

When immigration policies change, skilled professionals will be able to compare even more freely the prospects that await them abroad to the possibilities they face at home. In all likelihood, not only their access to foreign countries but also the welcomes they might expect as immigrants will have improved in many cases. The question is whether their own countries will be able to keep up.

Moreover, the growth that many poor countries have experienced as a result of globalization may be tapped out within a couple of decades. Much of it has depended on exporting commodities as demand from other fast-growing economies pushes up prices. The profits have tended to be concentrated among rulers and owners of property, not the farmhands who harvest crops or the miners who extract precious minerals.

This kind of lopsided growth does not lay the groundwork for future steps up the skills ladder, because the majority of the population can never climb above a subsistence wage. Nor does it create many opportunities for talented locals, since only a few doctors, engineers, and other professionals are needed by the elites. There's no cause to invest in laboratories for scientists, and there's no capital market to lend money to promising entrepreneurs.

In this situation, leaving will look increasingly attractive. Of course, only those people who already have a bit of money in their pockets will be able to cross the mountains, valleys, oceans, and rivers to pursue better opportunities. Right now, emigration rates for college-educated people from Sub-Saharan Africa and South Asia are eight times higher than for people with only a high school education. In those regions, people without a high school education basically do not emigrate at all.

If emigration becomes easier and even encouraged, inequality will worsen; the professional class will slowly disappear, and the very poor—who probably couldn't qualify for legal immigration anyway—will remain. With more inequality will come more instability, and even dimmer prospects for economic growth and social welfare. An urban, professional middle class has been a constant in economic growth in the late twentieth and early twenty-first centuries. Without it, countries tend to remain in a state of modern feudalism, with a small elite of wealthy landowners hoarding the country's wealth while the rest of the population lives in subsistence or servitude—a grinding injustice that can breed violent discontent, as it has across Latin America and Sub-Saharan Africa.

To lose that middle class, just as it is beginning to develop, would guarantee that poor but relatively progressive countries like Mozambique and Malawi would never see economic progress. The exodus could even derail the countries that are not yet investors' darlings but are still making meaningful strides in economic development, like Senegal and Peru. Truly, the opening of doors in rich countries could spell disaster for poor countries, whose citizens will walk right through.

THIS exacerbation of the brain drain ought to worry rich countries at least as much as their own demographically rooted challenges. To be sure, in the most cynical of scenarios they could take advantage of instability in poor countries by selling arms to the combatants in civil wars and border conflicts. But putting aside the obvious humanitarian concerns, peace would be even more in their interest. Peaceful countries can grow, and growing countries can buy imports from abroad.

The rich nations will be in a quandary. They will need immigrants to stoke the fires of their own economies, but by encouraging a brain drain from the developing world, they will risk causing even greater problems. Can they have both?

There are two possibilities. One is to exercise some self-control in immigration, perhaps by limiting the number of professionals who can arrive from countries where skills are scarce or by giving temporary permits that allow immigrants to make an economic contribution before returning home. This type of policy is difficult to maintain, however, because other countries might rush to pick up the slack; all wealthy countries eager to accept immigrants would have to commit to moderating their intake, like loggers pledging to leave a few tall trees in a forest that might otherwise be clear-cut. So far, there is no coalition working toward this goal, perhaps because the race to snap up the "best" immigrants has not yet broken into a sprint.

An alternative is to try to level the playing field by building up opportunities in poor countries. This policy has the potential to be win-win; fewer professionals might seek to emigrate, but the economic growth that would result could unlock myriad benefits for rich countries, too, as outlined above. To implement the policy, those rich countries would have to engineer a massive redistribution of resources and expertise, starting now. They would have to open their markets further to poor countries' products, offer their own corporations incentives to participate in joint ventures in the poor countries, build universities and training schools in the poor countries, and create partnerships between their own government agencies and those in the poor countries to improve public services, budgeting, and regulation. Doing so would make today's deficits even worse and leave less money for addressing the long-term pension problem—a real political challenge. In the long term, however, this might be the only way out. To date, rich countries have had trouble moving beyond square one, and, as discussed in the previous chapter, they still use a variety of barriers to block access to their markets.

Poor countries will have to make decisions, too. Will they allow their people to leave, or will they just focus on creating better opportunities for them at home? Will they let their people go abroad to study and build up their skills, even if those people might never come back? Countries like China, Syria, Cuba, and the Soviet Union and its satellites tried to limit emigration in the past, but it's not clear whether those policies helped their economies in the long term.

A third way might be to cooperate directly with individuals, offering opportunities to potential migrants that are win-win for rich and poor countries alike. For example, rich countries might offer extended visas for skilled workers that included a period of education or training, on the condition that these workers would return to help their countries of origin afterward. Some of them do so voluntarily, of course, but as the statistics quoted earlier showed, many do not. Rich countries might also require skilled migrants to send a portion of their incomes back to their home countries; indeed, remittances of this kind are already an important income support for some countries in Latin America and Southeast Asia. But, like the other options, these policies have not been implemented in any widespread fashion, either.

A lack of awareness of the coming challenges is surely part of the reason why none of these options has been pursued very seriously, but political incentives also play an important role. Most of the policies carry an up-front cost that only yields benefits over the long term: spending money to build capacity in poor countries, accepting migrant workers to reduce future generations' taxes, and investing in the training of migrants to help them turn their countries into future export markets. For most politicians, this is a difficult choice; they will suffer the political fallout from making unpopular choices, but they won't be in office a decade or two later, when the payoffs arrive. They will only be able to make these choices when their constituents realize the magnitude of the long-term risk their economies are facing: a failure to achieve, in their lifetimes, the potential that is their birthright.

5

THE BACKLASH AGAINST CAPITALISM
WON'T LAST, BUT IT WON'T BE REPLACED BY
POLITICAL STABILITY, EITHER.

Shortages of resources are not the only problem that can stop countries from realizing their economic potential. Political instability, if not the choice of an unhelpful political system, has long been an obstacle to robust growth. That instability can take many forms, from volatile democracy with frequent elections to domestic terrorism and all-out civil war.

At one extreme of the spectrum, civil war can be a huge hurdle for growth; during such a conflict, the country's resources are essentially being used to kill its own people instead of producing useful goods and services. But even peaceful instability can be an obstacle to growth; when a country's political regime changes frequently, the long succession of new governments can also create a succession of new policies and regulations, making planning more difficult for businesses. Sometimes, a change that ejects an ineffective government can unleash faster economic growth. Yet even in these cases, growth is usually put on hold during the period of instability that leads to the change.

The likelihood that political instability will occur (or continue) often has much to do with a country's starting position. Logically, governments whose policies reflect a national consensus are unlikely to be forcibly removed; those whose policies polarize their citizens and alienate large portions of the population are likely to run into trouble. In the latter situation, the gulf that divides people often has to do with a mix of ideology and economics: left versus right, liberals versus conservatives, rich versus poor.

The twentieth century was the setting for a battle of economic ideologies the likes of which the world had never seen. You could argue that mercantilism and internationalism had duked it out in the eighteenth century as colonialist powers fought for territory and trading routes. But nothing absorbed as many working hours, resources, and human lives as the battle between capitalism and communism, the Cold War.

That war was fought, according to typical chronologies, between the end of World War II in 1945 and the fall of the Berlin Wall in 1989. Yet the supposed finale of the Cold War really brought a redirection of motives rather than a definitive end to hostilities. One set of motives had to do with national pride and ambitions for a sphere of influence, and it has not disappeared. Russia still cherishes that pride and covets that influence in the neighborhood it formerly dominated; China still hopes to become a counterweight to American power; and the West continues to cultivate allies—democratic and othewise—in every corner of the world. The other set of motives was more directly economic: governments tried to enhance their countries' access to vital commodities, businesses sought new markets for their products, and people sought more equal distributions of wealth and better opportunities for themselves and their children.

During the Cold War, these two sets of motives were usually pursued together in lockstep. A country could become a Soviet satellite, receiving aid in the form of arms, money, and exports, and not adopt the Soviet economic system. Once a country did join, trade with the West was limited and strictly controlled. Now this has changed. Russia is cultivating an alliance with

Venezuela, whose economy is arguably much more socialist, at this point, than Russia's. And every year, the United States funnels millions of dollars' worth of food and other assistance to countries that are nominally socialist, such as North Korea and Laos. In the meantime, almost every country can, in principle, trade with every other country in the world.

Yet the clash of economic ideologies continues. Most wealthy countries continue to strike a balance between capitalism and socialism that leans strongly toward the former. Their governments may continue to be involved in some sectors of the economy—this is particularly true in small countries and in industries that require heavy investments in infrastructure, such as energy and telecommunications—but these countries shy away from central planning of the economy as practiced in the Soviet bloc and Mao Zedong's China. And though they may have a typically socialist-inspired combination of high, progressive tax rates and a generous system of social support, including free health care and education, they still try to ensure that individual workers receive rewards related to their efforts and abilities.

Among developing countries, there is more variation. Some were communist but switched to a form of capitalism almost overnight, as Poland did. Others, like Vietnam, are making the transition more gradually. A few countries have embraced laissez-faire capitalism and the divestiture of the state from the economy with unabashed enthusiasm; Chile moved so far toward pure capitalism that members of George W. Bush's administration proposed that its privatized pension program become a model for the United States.

Many others, having tried some version of the laissez-faire model, are now moving back to the left. Their swing amounts to more than just the election of a few center-left parties. Rather, movements from the hard left (especially in Latin America) and even former communists (especially in Eastern Europe) have been gaining ground and, in several cases, the highest office in the land. Some countries, like Argentina, Nicaragua, and Uruguay, have even chosen former revolutionary guerrillas to lead them after democratic elections.

Two main story lines explain this swing. In the first, countries that suffered under decades of corrupt and oligarchic capitalism finally decided they'd had enough. The disenchantment and disgust were usually deepened by the failure of the government, often a center-right affair led by politicians intimately related to the country's main business interests, to improve the lot of the poor and to fend off domestic economic crises. These countries might have grown quickly for a while, but that growth only widened gaps in income between the traditionally wealthy classes and the rest of the people. The people who were already rich and well educated had a leg up when it came to exploiting the opportunities created by globalization in the past quarter-century. Populists trumpeting socialist-sounding slogans successfully appealed to the working classes and carried some left-leaning intellectuals along with them. They came to power, usually in democratic elections, and set about consolidating their power.

Bolivia, whose center-right, pro-business government was forced out in 2003 after protests against exports of the country's natural resources, is a case in point. Between the adoption of a liberal, pro-business economic policy in the mid-1980s and 2003, Bolivia's average income grew by just 0.7 percent per year, adjusted for inflation. Inequality shot up in the last few years of the pro-business government of Gonzalo Sánchez de Lozada, placing Bolivia among the ten most unequal countries in the world. After protests led to bloody riots, he left the country. He was succeeded by two presidents not aligned with any political party, who served brief terms before Bolivia elected Sánchez de Lozada's polar opposite, Evo Morales, in 2005. Morales, a populist who wanted to implement a socialist government in the style of Venezuela's Hugo Chávez, had been a leader of the protests that had resulted in Sánchez de Lozada's resignation and flight.

In the second story line, countries that had embraced capitalism in recent years found themselves falling without a net when the global financial crisis hit. Twenty years after the fall of the Berlin Wall supposedly pronounced the final verdict on communism, the destruction of trillions of dollars of essentially fictional wealth seemed to do the same for capitalism. In these countries, faith in capitalism was shaken and economic conditions worsened, sending many people into the welcoming arms of socialist politicians who promised free health care, job security, and state pensions. In other countries, the economic crisis only amplified previous grievances stemming from other problems perceived as failures of capitalism: the mistaken policies recommended by the International Monetary Fund in Latin America and East Asia in the wake of the wave of crises that began in the 1980s, the injustices of trading rules ushered in by the World Trade Organization, and the bullying of small countries with underdeveloped legal systems by multinational corporations.

The about-face from capitalism to socialism occurred most starkly in Moldova, where eleven years of pro-capitalist governments were followed, from 2001 to 2009, by three communist governments. The earlier transition from communism to a market-driven economy had brought as many problems as benefits. Crippled by corruption, rampant inflation, and mismanaged privatizations, the economy shrank for several years during the 1990s, until, according to the World Bank, 60 percent of gross domestic product had essentially disappeared. With their living standards under capitalism so much lower than under communism, Moldovans brought back the party of their former authoritarian masters.

These bizarre turnarounds, which took place over the course of just two decades, served to illustrate one axiom that will guide this discussion: neither unrestrictedly capitalist nor completely communist economic systems are sustainable in the long term.

———————

UNRESTRICTED capitalism damns itself because it provides a blueprint for a world that doesn't exist: a world where the market never fails, where economic opportunity is equally distributed, and where all the inhabitants are happy to play by the rules. Capitalism can't work on its own when, for example, using a product has harmful side effects, like the pollution caused by driving oversized sport utility vehicles. Even a basic economic analysis shows that consumers won't fully take into account these side effects when they buy these products, unless the government intervenes to change their incentives, for example, by taxing SUVs.

Capitalism can also create problems on the supply side of markets. Though many avowed lovers of capitalism are also devoted to the idea of competition, the two do not always go together. If left completely to their own devices, companies that grow quickly in a capitalist system can throw up barriers to prevent others from competing with them for market share, eventually turning themselves into monopolies that gouge consumers and leave the market constricted and unsatisfied. This is why most capitalist countries have some kind of anti-trust regulation.

But capitalism also comes up short in important ways that these same countries have failed to address. Protecting the process of competition can create very imperfect economic results. For example, consider markets where there are two dominant companies fighting for market share. If one outspends the other on advertising, it will gain the loyalty of more consumers. But if both spend as much as they can, their market shares won't actually change. The same would be true if both companies spent very little on advertising, though they can't coordinate to do that—each one would always have an incentive to break the deal. The problem is that the massive spending on advertising—think of Coke and Pepsi—implies an enormous

waste of time and resources that could be used more productively somewhere else in the economy.

Another major failure of capitalism is in workplace training. Technology is advancing rapidly these days, so the content
of jobs changes quickly. Old jobs disappear, and new jobs are
created. In the meantime, labor markets continue to become
more flexible and dynamic; hiring and firing is easier for employers; and switching jobs is also easier for employees. In this
context, training and retraining are more essential than ever.
Yet there is little incentive for companies to invest in enhancing
their workers' skills if the companies cannot be sure the workers will stay. As the recent economic downturn in the United
States hit bottom in early 2009, a survey of 141 large companies found that roughly half had either cut training programs
or planned to do so in the coming year. Training programs
can't be justified if trained employees leave, or if they have to
be let go.

There are some exceptions. In European soccer, big teams
pay a fee to smaller teams when they sign the smaller teams' up-
and-coming players; the fee depends on the player's potential,
which has presumably been enhanced by learning the game at
a lesser club. Some American companies will pay to train their
workers for executive positions—for example, by sending them
to obtain master's degrees in business administration—and then
require the workers to refund the cost if they decide not to
return to their jobs after finishing their schooling. This mechanism can result in a kind of market for training, since workers
considering a switch to new jobs could ask their new companies to make the payoff instead of making it themselves. But
mechanisms like this are relatively uncommon. At the top of
the skills ladder, companies are reluctant to sue employees
who leave after their training; doing so would be costly and
might result in bad publicity. At the bottom, long and costly
training programs are rare; those that do exist may not be
worth the trouble of creating a contractual mechanism.

Until there are more ways to coordinate the financing of training, it will be undersupplied in capitalist economies—and perhaps further from an efficient level than it would be in more centrally planned economies. The effect of this under-supply will be to widen the skills gap between high-earning and low-earning workers, engendering greater inequality over time.

Capitalism also falls down if it assumes a level playing field, when it's obvious that not everyone is born with the same chances for economic success. Creating a regulatory environment that offers every business a chance doesn't mean that every prospective entrepreneur has the same education, start-up capital, and connections. The recent wave of globalization has complicated this situation even further, since it has generated opportunities that are most easily exploited by people who already hold strong positions in the global economy. Not surprisingly, even as income differences between countries have narrowed, income differences within countries have widened. Without assertive measures to redistribute the material gains of globalization, this tendency will only amplify itself.

Moreover, as the recent excesses on Wall Street and across the world's financial markets have clearly shown, even the capitalists with all the advantages—the most sophisticated people in the system—cannot always be trusted to make decisions that are in their own interests, let alone society's interests. The problem is not just one of greed, herd behavior, negligence, or loopholes in the system; it is also a mismatch of time horizons. As a whole, society usually targets a time horizon that is a generation or two away, for example, leaving its children a better standard of living. Today's capitalists have a much shorter one: next quarter's earnings report, next month's bonus. It stands to reason that their choices place a premium on a quick buck, even if doing so threatens society's future.

Unrestricted capitalism, therefore, can cause a raft of problems: market failures that increase inequality, opportunities taken by people with more resources or connections rather than more talent, decisions made for the short term rather than to maximize long-term economic potential. Left to operate for long enough in almost any country, this combination would eventually create a vast underclass and a never-ending boom-bust cycle that damaged society and the natural environment as well. At that point, the question would become whether the haves could control the resentment of the have-nots by throwing them enough bones and scraps to avoid a revolt. The many earlier backlashes against relatively unrestricted capitalism, from the union movement in the United States to the popular revolutions across Latin America, Africa, and Asia, offer convincing evidence that the haves usually can't keep this up forever. The backlashes don't always last, either, as we will see later.

Communism offers a political and economic system that is equally vulnerable to capitalism, as the unraveling of the Soviet bloc demonstrated. Put simply, a country living with communist values isn't robust enough to withstand an invasion of noncommunist values. A useful analogy comes from the nexus of ecology and evolutionary biology, which studies how communities of bacteria, animals, and plants can be disrupted by the appearance of an outsider or a mutant. For example, a community of hawks might not be threatened by the introduction of a few doves. Most likely, the doves would be swiftly cowed or even eaten. Not so for the introduction of a few hawks into a community of doves: the hawks would probably thrive and multiply until they, not the doves, were the majority.

In virtually every country whose government has tried to maintain a communist system—be it of the strictly Marxist-Leninist, Stalinist, or Maoist variety—the intrusion of noncommunist goods, culture, and ideas has eroded the faith of the populace in that system. It is human nature to see the glamorous trappings of a foreign society and to aspire to or desire them, no matter how illusory they might in fact be. Only the most isolated and authoritarian countries, like North Korea, have managed to keep foreign intrusions to a minimum. Economically they have lagged far behind their neighbors in the past half-century.

Part of the reason for that lag has been the countries' isolation from the rest of the world. By blocking out the foreign influences that might have undermined their forms of government, they also curtailed possibilities for useful exchanges of ideas and technology. And the economic lag has worsened because of a deeper problem: the difficulty of depending on central planning as a way of organizing the economy. Economies have millions, even billions, of moving parts: people, companies, markets, and the decisions that all of them make for the future. Although a government might try to guide the behavior of these moving parts in broad strokes, trying to control the parts one by one to maximize productivity is a tall task. The planned surges of industrialization in the Soviet Union and China in the 1950s yielded impressive results in the short term, but the countries soon stumbled to growth rates that were below those of capitalist nations—and even further below the growth rates they achieved when they began to open up to the world and allow limited forms of free enterprise to flourish.

Efficient central planning requires a kind of omniscience that no government can have. It also requires a popular commitment to the national economic project that supersedes the problematic individual incentives created by a communist system. In a system where everyone has the same standard of living regardless of individual effort, people must have some other reason to work besides direct personal gain, such as a chance to show the superiority of their ideology. Yet in the second half of the twentieth century, no communist country was able to match the living standards in the wealthier capitalist nations. Even if people are committed to the national project, no one likes to be a loser, which may be why the government of North Korea must constantly tell its people that they are winners and followers of the one true path, just as governments behind the Iron Curtain did before it fell.

LET'S return to the current swing to the left in Latin America and Eastern Europe. Right now, it seems that several countries in these regions could be moving closer to socialism for many years to come. Current tendencies, however, do not always turn into long-term trends. People have to make decisions along the way, and changes in economic and social conditions can lead them to choose different leaders and policies—even if those changes were caused by the leaders and policies they chose in the past. The dynamics of these shifts depend as much on human nature as on traditional economics. Logic, rather than extrapolation, is the key to understanding what will happen.

First, let's say the socialist reforms of the new, left-leaning leaders are successful. The fortunes of the poor are measurably improved, their children grow up healthy and well educated, and the next generation of workers is more productive than any that came before. Assuming their country still participates in international trade, these workers' higher productivity will probably translate into higher wages, because they will be able to produce higher-value goods and services to sell on global markets. Their government, in turn, ensures that much of the revenue from those exports is reinvested equitably in the country's future. Soon enough, a poor and unequal country has become a middle-income if not exactly wealthy place, with a much more even distribution of wealth. This could happen, hypothetically, in a country like Ecuador, where the highest-earning 10 percent of urban households received a whopping 43 percent of the income in 2007; its president, Rafael Correa, is an ally of Venezuela's Hugo Chávez who has pledged to help the poor.

Then what happens? With things going well so far, would a country like Ecuador continue moving toward a communist ideal by nationalizing industries, making virtually everyone an employee of the state, and setting production targets in the halls of government? Let's say it does, and all the citizens are pleased with the country's progress and committed to the national project. Great, right? Not quite. We know that continuing down this road could have disastrous consequences. A completely communist government is expected to provide employment and support for all of its people, a tough task if the economy should ever drift into recession. And central planning of any economy is a difficult job; setting wages, prices, and production targets, then rationing goods and services, has been tried in capitalist and communist countries alike. Though organizing a country's industrial capacity with the government's help can foster economic growth in some cases—Japan, South Korea, and Taiwan enjoyed some success along these lines—it has never worked in the long term. As an economy grows and begins to diversify, that kind of control can be difficult and costly to maintain.

More likely, the country in question would settle into the kind of social democracy that could be seen across much of Western Europe a few decades ago: a strong social safety net, deeply progressive income taxes, government domination of a few key industries, a high percentage of employment in the public sector, and a relatively heavy regulatory regime for business. Even that system, however, has proved vulnerable. The United Kingdom discarded it in large part after Margaret Thatcher became prime minister in 1979; she led a wave of privatizations and deregulation while pummeling the country's once-powerful labor unions. Sweden, once touted as a social democratic utopia, elected center-right governments in 1991 and 2006, and the government has steadily divested from the country's major industries. Denmark, which has one of the most generous programs of social support in the world, also has a center-right government—and it supported the exploits of the United States in both Afghanistan and Iraq. At the time of this writing, center-right governments were in power in Germany, France, and Italy. All three countries were once much closer to socialism; the state had a much larger role in their economies, and the workers in major industries were represented by powerful unions. That role and those unions diminished with time, however, as the countries consolidated their wealth in a peaceful setting. They didn't become as overtly capitalist as the United States purports to be, but as they became wealthier the workers decided they didn't need to be so militant or so dependent on their government.

If things do not go well, of course, a much more dangerous and uncertain path awaits these left-leaning economies. In the case of democratic countries, an initial socialist mandate, if it fails to yield tangible results for the well-being of the majority, may simply be replaced in the next election. For countries that have moved further down the road to true state socialism, the pitfalls are many. Failed central planning can lead to shortages (if a country becomes economically isolated and does not produce enough on its own), runaway inflation (if a government tries to cover its debts by printing money), wasting of talent (if workers are not allowed to choose their own jobs or develop their own ideas), and overall stunting of growth (if what is left of the private sector cannot organize itself through mergers and strategic partnerships or innovate on its own). All of these problems are likely to leave people poorer, unsatisfied, and looking for new leadership. Additionally, it is much more difficult now—and it will become even more difficult in the future—to keep people isolated from outside influences than it was decades ago, when the first socialist governments emerged.

With dissent mounting in tandem with economic problems, a slow move toward socialism could be followed by a rapid change of government, culminating in who-knows-what kind of political system. Just ask the former members of the Soviet

Union's sphere of influence, which disintegrated in a sequence of peaceful transitions and popular revolts. Many of them founded stable democracies and entered the European Union; others ended up with dictators such as Saparmurat Niyazov of Turkmenistan, who decided to rename the months of the year for himself and members of his family.

So, if socialism works, it is unlikely to last in a pure form. If it doesn't work, then it certainly won't last. It seems like a pretty open-and-shut case. Yet there are two exceptions to these predictions.

The first exception, demonstrated by North Korea, is rather uninteresting from an economic perspective. It only shows that a completely authoritarian government can institute whatever economic system it wants, maintaining that system in a setting of international isolation and at the cost of thousands of lives (lost, in North Korea's case, to hunger and prison camps). It certainly does not show socialism as a route to higher living standards; life expectancy there is under sixty-four years, among the worst in the world. Cuba, another example of socialism under an authoritarian system, does not have as tragic a record of human suffering, and it has made progress in educating its people and keeping them healthy. In the United Nations' Human Development Index, it ranks 51st—above Mexico, Brazil, and even some of the newer members of the European Union. Yet it still lags behind those same countries in terms of its people's average purchasing power, at 108th in the world. It is also important to note that both countries received substantial financial and material support from their ideological torchbearers in the Soviet Union and China. Without that support, they might not have achieved even these results.

The second exception is supplied by Venezuela, a country pursuing socialism with the cushion of a substantial native source of income. In 2007, Venezuela sold over two million barrels of oil a day on world markets, which would translate to about $54 billion at the year's average price of $68 per barrel.

This amount was equivalent to more than half of the government's budget and 85 percent of the country's money supply. The money allowed the government to invest in education, public health, and other social programs, constructing the basis of the safety net that socialist governments are supposed to provide. The Venezuelan government also began nationalizing and re-nationalizing dominant companies in industries other than petroleum, like steel and cement, usually to the dismay of their overseas owners. If productivity in those industries dropped while under government control, the oil and gas revenue would probably still pick up the slack.

Yet this approach has dangers, too. When oil and gas prices change, as they did with the onset of the global financial crisis, years of budget planning can go out the window almost overnight. Before the crisis, in July 2008, oil prices had maxed out around $145 per barrel. In early 2009, with oil prices hovering around $40, Venezuela cut its budget by 6.7 percent and announced increases in sales taxes. Even when prices were high, there were risks for Venezuela; pumping so much money from exports into an economy can create a real danger of inflation, especially if the output of goods and services is not rising at the same time. The reason is simple: you have more and more cash in the hands of consumers but no change in the quantity of products they can buy, so naturally they bid up those products' prices. In 2007, the inflation rate in Venezuela was 19 percent, and it rose to 30 percent in 2008.

A government can offset this risk somewhat by keeping the economy open to imports, thus giving consumers an almost infinite supply of things to buy. But in that situation, standards of living become heavily linked to exchange rates, which can be very volatile; people may be tempted to start keeping their money overseas, where it adds nothing to their home country's capacity to grow. In addition, keeping a country open allows in all those outside influences that could erode people's faith in the socialist model.

A more subtle danger of the resource-based socialism of
Venezuela is that other countries may be encouraged to follow
the same model, yet without the luxury of the same natural
wealth. Venezuela's president, Hugo Chávez, has eagerly supported the duplication of his model in countries throughout
Latin America, with his allies taking up leadership posts in
Bolivia, Ecuador, Honduras, and Nicaragua. Like Venezuela,
these countries also depend heavily on exports, which amount
to at least a third of gross domestic product in all of them. But
their populations' living standards are also much lower, on
average, than Venezuela's, as the following chart shows:

PURCHASING POWER PER CAPITA IN DOLLAR TERMS, 2009

Venezuela	$13,100
Ecuador	7,400
Bolivia	4,600
Honduras	4,200
Nicaragua	2,800

SOURCE: U.S. Central Intelligence Agency, *World Factbook 2010*

What happens if these countries enter a recession, or if
world prices for the products they export suddenly drop? Since
their people are poorer, the effects will be felt much more deeply
than in Venezuela if their governments have to scale back spending. How will the governments be able to continue paying for
social services and keep guaranteeing employment to their citizens, if indeed socialism has progressed far enough to grant
governments that responsibility? At the time of this writing,
the wealthiest of these countries, Ecuador, had a sovereign
credit rating of CCC+, meaning that it was virtually impossible for its government to borrow money at a reasonable rate on
international markets—a situation that would become even
tougher if its economy were in trouble. Most likely, these governments would have to cut back spending in vital areas, a

measure that would be necessary (unless another country, like Venezuela, comes to the rescue with a big loan) but extremely difficult to bear in lean times. Mass poverty and unemployment could return, with the political consequences uncertain at best.

FOR socialism to grow in influence, it needs popular support. You wouldn't expect an elite ruling class to impose socialist measures voluntarily, giving up their own riches and their control of industry and commerce. If the majority of a population is against a move to the left (or further to the left), it probably won't happen. And as that majority becomes better educated, better fed, better taken care of, and better informed, the allure of all-out socialism is likely to diminish—perhaps not for all of them, but for enough of them to make a difference.

   This dynamic is the result of natural human tendencies. Socialism has sprouted in places where two kinds of privation are present: absolute and relative. Under absolute privation, people lack the basics needed to survive: food, shelter, and medical care. They have little to lose and everything to gain by switching to a socialist system, where at least these things will be provided. These people also suffer privation in relative terms; they look at wealthier people in their country, and perhaps at people in wealthier countries around the world, and they want what those people have. Yet when relative privation exists by itself, it is not always enough to push people toward socialism, and it is certainly not enough to make socialism stick. Rather, in middle- and high-income countries where the majority of the population is gainfully employed under a capitalist system, relative privation—not having as fancy a car as your boss, for example—is usually accepted by that same majority.

   By its very nature, absolute privation begins to disappear as living standards improve, taking away the main rationale for socialism. Those who would foment socialism are left with relative privation as a motivator. But relative privation can take different forms, too. Some people may favor the socialist ideal, using the resources saved by doing without fancy cars to build more schools and hospitals. But others might be happy enough with their schools and hospitals; they just want the fancy cars for themselves. They also want the enormous television screens, the beautiful clothes, and the airline tickets to exotic places— all the things popular culture so skillfully tells them to want. How could they possibly get those luxuries in a socialist system? A traditional socialist system wouldn't even allow such luxuries to exist, since producing them uses up too many resources that could instead be devoted to necessities. Indeed, those luxuries are only produced in capitalist countries, and, more important, only capitalist countries allow their citizens to become so wealthy—so much wealthier than their fellow citizens—that they can obtain them. In short, even relative privation is an unreliable motivator for socialism once countries attain a reasonably high standard of living.

By this logic, the wealthier countries now experiencing a backlash against capitalism may swing slightly to the left, but they will be unlikely to go further than the social democracies in Europe, and eventually they will swing back toward the right, as those countries did. The poorer countries involved in this trend will take longer to make this transition; Nicaragua, for example, may actually stay on the left longer than Venezuela.

IF we accept the notion that the current backlash against capitalism will not last, where does that leave us? It is certainly possible that such a backlash will recur in the future. Indeed, the history of the world is full of political cycles that swing from left to right and back again, even centuries before Karl Marx and Friedrich Engels were born. In many cases, those cycles crested in violent revolutions by an oppressed under-class, occasionally successfully (as in the slave revolt that led to the founding of the Haitian Republic) and many times unsuc-cessfully, despite much bloodshed (as in the Paris Commune).

We see these cycles not just in poor countries ruled by des-potic elites but also in democracies. The revolutionary move-ments in Latin America and Africa have analogs in the Black Panther movement in the United States of the 1970s and the French riots of 2005. The French rioters were a particularly interesting case; many were young people who received income support and benefits from the state, and they could live fairly comfortable lives. That wasn't enough, however—they wanted jobs. Even when people have the vote, even when they have places to live, health care, and schools, they still want some-thing more: real opportunity to improve their lives and those of their families, and a chance to hold a stake in the society in which they live.

In spite of this basic truth, countries around the world con-tinue to take only small steps to reduce poverty and create equal economic opportunities for all. As a result, the cycle con-tinues. In most years, the handouts are enough to keep the poor and disadvantaged quiet. Once in a while, they rebel. But at any given time, that prospect probably seems quite remote to the people in power; as they think about the next election or perhaps about enriching themselves from the national trea-sury, they would rather skimp in the short term than worry too much about the long-term consequences.

Yet these cycles are undoubtedly costly. Times of civil unrest are usually unproductive economically: people who might be supplying goods and services are engaged in fighting instead; resources are diverted to pay for arms and ammunition, which serve no productive purpose; infrastructure may be damaged or destroyed during battle; and liquidity disappears as foreign-ers pull investment funds out of the country and locals stuff their own money under the mattress. In addition, to the extent that the cycles are the product of a broad polarization in the incomes of the rich and the poor, the talents of the poor may be underutilized over the course of the cycle, resulting in a loss to the economy as a whole.

Furthermore, civil unrest need not be violent to be economically costly. A tense climate can be enough to scare off potential investors and dissuade businesses from hiring more people or building up their physical plant. The problem is uncertainty; you can't think ahead several moves into the game if the rules might change at any moment.

So, how can a country exit this cycle, given the shortness of political time horizons? The answer lies not just in distributing handouts but in making lasting changes to the economic landscape. Capitalism is most sustainable and requires the least fine-tuning when there is equality of opportunity. Socialism begins to stall when the government controls the economy too closely. In almost every area of the economy, countries must strike a balance: in labor markets, between job security and the ability of companies to hire and fire easily; in social supports, between assuring a decent standard of living and removing the incentive to work; in industrial policy, between coordinating growth to compete in export markets and entrenching collusive practices. The countries that choose extremes instead will probably continue to swing from one side to another like so many pendulums, losing ground all the while in the race for higher living standards.

PART III

OPPORTUNITIES

6

AMERICANS WILL BECOME THE WORLD'S SALES FORCE.

Just as there are obstacles on the path to growth, there are also opportunities: new industries to promote, new jobs to take, new hubs for economic activity, and new gains from trade. Exploiting these opportunities does not necessarily push back the limits of growth—you can't change your economy's ultimate potential without changing the deep factors discussed in part I—but it can help you to reach those limits more quickly.

Because so much of economic growth depends on innovation, predicting which forces will propel countries to higher living standards in the future can be a dicey business. Experts who forecast that Japan would pass the United States in terms of economic might were proved wrong, not just because the Japanese bubble burst and left the country's economy in pieces for a decade, but also because they didn't foresee the American productivity boom of the 1990s. The mass adoption of transformative technologies like personal computers, mobile phones, and the Internet would have been difficult to imagine for anyone, except perhaps a science-fiction writer.

Now, as the global economy and its biggest national economy, the United States, face the prospect of an extended period of average or sub-par growth, economists and investors are understandably casting around for the next big thing. This question hasn't been asked in the United States since the 1980s, and it is an uncomfortable one for economists and politicians alike. At first, green technology seemed like a potential savior, but we quickly realized (1) it probably wasn't big enough to drive an enormous economy like the United States, and (2) the United States certainly wouldn't have a monopoly on it.

There are less sexy, more reliable ways to increase economic growth in the long term. As part of its efforts to stimulate the American economy, the government of Barack Obama did hand out billions of dollars of subsidies for green business, but it also went back to tried-and-true sources of growth like education and basic scientific research. These were probably two of the biggest sources of American growth in the second half of the twentieth century, spurred on by the Cold War and, more specifically, the space race. But those investments can take a generation to pay off, so it is hard for politicians to commit to sustaining them. Also, thanks to rapid growth in the developing world, the United States is facing more competition than ever before as it tries to transform education and research into marketable products and new jobs.

With this gloomy prognosis, you might ask what, if anything, will continue to make the American economy special. Is there some magic ingredient, some special sauce that will prevent the economy from receding into respectable anonymity among the world's leading economic pack, the way Britain did in the nineteenth and early twentieth centuries?

THE American advantage used to be the way Americans did business: free markets, low levels of corruption, high levels of trust, a willingness to accept risk, a taste for entrepreneurship, a political system that never strayed too far from the middle ground, and a legal framework that offered solid protections for investors, consumers, and small business owners. These deep factors made the United States a safe place to put your money and a good place to do business. Yet they are not as big an advantage as they used to be.

You wouldn't expect these deep factors to change very much from year to year in any country, and perhaps least of all in the United States; you don't mess with a good thing. Other countries, however, have been trying to improve their deep factors and thus expand their potential to reach higher material living standards. Some, like the Soviet Union's former republics and satellites, got the chance to start with a clean slate. Others have done it through long campaigns to change their business culture and economic environment through new policies, education, and legal action. An interesting example of these phenomena is Georgia. In 2004, more than a decade after the dissolution of the Soviet Union but just after the Rose Revolution ushered in a more representative form of democracy, Georgia still ranked a dismal 133rd out of 145 countries in Transparency International's Corruption Perceptions Index. The next year, the Georgian government put in place a comprehensive and highly publicized anti-corruption strategy. By 2009, its rank in the index had risen to 66 out of 180, better than three members of the European Union.

Catch-up in the deep factors would eliminate the differences that give the United States a higher limit for growth, taking away its advantages in attracting resources, financial capital, and talented people from around the world. Even American companies have already begun a mass exodus in search of friendlier corporate climes, relocating not just their mailing addresses but also their executives, researchers, and product designers abroad to join their offshore production workers. Big made-in-America names like Accenture (formerly Andersen Consulting), Ingersoll-Rand, Tyco International, and Noble Drilling have moved their headquarters to Bermuda, the Cayman Islands, and Switzerland to dodge American taxes and financial regulations.

In the meantime, the American manufacturing sector continues to become less labor-intensive. Despite the quintupling of its output since 1960, manufacturing has shed roughly three million jobs. In fact, multinational companies have found they can distribute the various parts of their operations in the countries that suit them best: manufacturing in countries with copious cheap labor, customer service in countries with low-wage English speakers, back office in countries with an underpaid but educated professional class, and headquarters in a tax haven. This trend will continue, and the question will echo again from the point of view of the American worker: what will I do to make a living ten, twenty, or thirty years from now?

Consider how the next generation is preparing to enter the workforce. Since the early 1970s, the distribution of college majors has changed only slightly. In the 1970–1971 academic year, 44 percent of students were preparing for jobs in service industries; in 2006–2007, that percentage had risen to 48 percent. Over the same period, the percentage of science majors rose to 13 percent from 9 percent, but the percentage of engineering and technology majors was unchanged at 9 percent. The overall number of bachelor's degrees granted rose by more than 80 percent, to 1.5 million, though the nation's population grew by only 45 percent.

These changes don't point toward more jobs in the manufacturing sector; you don't necessarily need a college degree to work in manufacturing, and you certainly wouldn't be preparing for a service job if you were heading for the production line. Nor would you be studying a foreign language, and the share of American high school graduates with at least two years of foreign language training rose from about 10 percent in 1982 to more than 50 percent in 2005.

So, if the American worker's future lies in the service sector, what kinds of jobs will proliferate? The aging of the American population makes health care a good bet. As the baby boomers retire—the first of them turned sixty-five in 2010—they will need people to take care of them. A generation ago, they might have been able to count on their families to pitch in with this task. Now, with a much higher percentage of Americans working, caring for elderly loved ones in the home has often become a paying job. More home health aides will be needed, but also more doctors, nurses, and medical technicians—and for many years to come. The demographic bulge will still be present decades from now, partly because people will simply be living longer. At the time of this writing, there were 4.8 Americans between eighteen and sixty-four for each person sixty-five or older; by 2040, there will be only 2.8.

Another safe bet is that there will be more jobs in education. Americans will need more and more education to compete in the global economy, especially if they want to continue to have average incomes among the highest in the world. For every Bill Gates who drops out of college and becomes a billionaire, thousands of Americans become innovators after years of necessary training. You'd have a very hard time developing new biotechnological treatments for cancer, for example, if you'd never studied biochemistry at the graduate level. There is an opportunity to create jobs here because Americans still start out just as educated as the first human beings who walked the earth—that is, not knowing anything—so more education means spending more years in school. Some Americans will try to develop new ways of learning to cut down that schooling time, but many more will be teachers and administrators.

Right now, more people are working in health care than in manufacturing, and almost as many work in education as in manufacturing. Not surprisingly, the Bureau of Labor Statistics has forecast that the occupations showing the most growth in the coming decade for people without advanced degrees will be heavily concentrated in health care and education. Office work— essentially, providing support for all the service jobs—will also be a big source of job growth. And this is all very well; these are useful jobs that help to make the entire economy more productive, since they take care of and enhance the abilities of individual workers. However, these jobs have one shortcoming: most of what they produce is difficult to export. The jobs serve the American market and serve it well, but that's all.

One other occupation came through in spades in the bureau's report, and it was more of a surprise: sales—in fact, everything to do with sales and selling. Jobs for market research analysts were projected to rise by 41 percent from 2008 to 2018, versus overall job growth of about 10 percent; jobs for public relations specialists were projected to rise by 24 percent; management jobs in advertising, 13 percent; even jobs for models, 16 percent; the list went on. And therein flickered a glimmer of hope for the American worker.

THIS boom in sales-related occupations may seem paradoxical, since the supposed trend in retailing has been away from bricks-and-mortar stores and toward the Internet. Yet the proportion of the labor force working in sales has stayed remarkably steady since the early 1980s, when the Census Bureau began to compile data on occupations, and the Bureau of Labor Statistics predicts it will soon increase.

Why should this be the case? There are three possible reasons. One is that Americans are finding new ways to sell things to each other. Another is that Americans are starting to sell things to people outside of the United States. And the third is that Americans are very, very good at selling.

Now, you may say that people all over the world are good at selling. Markets and high streets everywhere are full of hawkers and hagglers. But there is one thing that the United States has that other people don't: American culture.

By its very nature, American culture is particularly suited to commercial application. The reason for this lies in American culture's very particular origins. The settlers of the United States erased much of the indigenous culture that had existed for many centuries, massacring the Native Americans or shunting them off to reservations. What remnants of their culture stayed behind were inevitably mixed with, and generally overwhelmed by, the influences of the new Americans' roots: English, Dutch, French, German, Scottish, Spanish, and African. No single one of these influences could monopolize American culture; they had to coexist, and they were bound to rub up against one another and commingle.

To be sure, one of these influences could dominate the others within a single community, especially if that community isolated itself from others of differing origins. But a culture that isolated itself would be commercially impotent. As the United States began to industrialize—at first replacing artisanal one-offs with products made from interchangeable parts, and later replacing workshops with assembly lines—its citizens learned about the wonders of economies of scale in manufacturing. They could begin to dream of enormous markets for their goods—not just their community or their town, but their whole state or even the whole country. To appeal to the whole country, however, would require a more generic culture, one that sought and found the lowest common denominator in every community, regardless of its roots.

Against this backdrop arose classic American hucksterism. It appealed to the lowest common denominator, selling products with extravagant claims of how they would enhance beauty, save time, improve health, and create wealth. And again, because of the uniqueness of American society, that lowest common denominator was very common indeed. The average American, if such a person can be said to have existed, was interested in self-improvement and success.

These were the very motivations that compelled so many people to arrive upon the shores of the young nation, and the language through which these motivations were expressed was just as direct and accessible to the average American as a P. T. Barnum sideshow. Consider the campaign of the Red River

Colony of Minnesota, a fairly barren patch of land trying to attract settlers in the mid-nineteenth century. An advertisement placed in *Harper's Weekly* declared that the colony's climate was "unsurpassed in its inspiriting, health-giving qualities" but warned that only settlers possessed of "Good standing at home, intelligence, and frugality" would be considered for "membership."

Commercial culture was also a particularly logical extension of the essential organization of American society. As a nation of immigrants, the United States placed much less importance on traditional ideas of aristocracy or high birth. Certainly, some families considered themselves superior to others because of their name or tenure on American soil. But this type of social order was much less prevalent than in the countries the Americans came from—Europe, Africa, and Asia. In the United States, then as now, money equaled class. If you had enough money, it didn't matter where you came from; providing you came by that money reasonably honestly, you could inspire a degree of unbegrudging reverence from your fellow citizens. They, after all, were aiming to end up like you.

The commercial culture echoed this notion of mobility with the aspirational tone of its advertising and marketing, a tone still present in the late-night television infomercials of today. It also echoed American culture in its embrace of a meritocratic egalitarianism. There was no reason why a millionaire and a paperboy shouldn't use the same hair tonic, and no reason why a society doyenne and a washerwoman shouldn't use the same garter belts. If those were the best products on the market, mass-produced with the latest technology and sold at low cost, then they were good enough for anyone. Celebrity endorsements, a natural manifestation of this idea, soon began to appear. One advertisement in *Harper's Weekly* for Vin Mariani, a cocaine-based tonic popular in the 1870s, featured a smiling photo of the well-known French actor and singer Jean-

François Berthelier. Another ad bore the image and endorse-
ment of no less a personage than Pope Leo XIII.

Any observer could see that American society was not perfectly meritocratic, but by selling the idea that it was, the commercial culture was also selling a small piece of the American
Dream. Perhaps you couldn't live every day like a millionaire,
but you sure could use the same hair tonic and, for one moment
every morning, picture yourself in his shoes.

The fact that this culture was built, for practical reasons, in
a way that paralleled an egalitarian, meritocratic ideal gave it
one more important attribute. When an American achieved
success by tapping the mass market, that success did not discourage or dim the prospects of any other American. On the
contrary, that success could be held up as an example that aspi-
rations could become reality. The promise of a life full of beauty
and leisure—the same life promised by nineteenth-century
products like B. T. Babbitt's Labor-Saving Union Soap—came
ever closer, and the sales pitch used to hawk that life's supposed trappings gained an ever more brilliant sheen of verisi-
militude.

These aspects of the American commercial culture also
made it incredibly flexible. Successive generations of immigrants could be integrated seamlessly into its markets. The
pitch was the same for the Irish and Italians as it was for the
English and Dutch. Of course, they added bits of their own
cultures into the mix, bringing with them goods and services
that had not yet existed in the United States, from Italian pizza
to Irish pumpkins for Halloween. And when they did, the flexibility of the commercial culture became an asset twice over;
not only could it incorporate these people into the market as
consumers, but it could adapt itself to their products, offering
all consumers something new with each wave of immigrants.

The commercial culture thus became not just aspirational
and flexible, but also self-perpetuating. There was always a

new product to buy or a new fashion to follow. As a result, the workers and factories producing the goods for the mass market had to become flexible, too. Indeed, you could argue that the modern, dynamic American worker was forged in the crucible of the nation's nascent commercial culture.

At about the same time as this identity was being formed, new mass media and communications technologies were also spreading across the United States: telephone lines, widely distributed films, radio transmissions, national newspapers, and television. These advances not only helped to expand the potential market for new products, but also made finding the lowest common denominator an even more powerful strategy. Local vendors could start to sell across the country—the Interstate Commerce Act of 1887 had laid the groundwork for them many years before—but they needed to make a pitch that would resonate beyond the borders of their town or state.

With all of these pieces in place, the American experience was unique. In the middle of the twentieth century, no other country could claim a population as diverse as that of the United States, a similar penetration of new technologies, and the same freedom of commerce across its territory. Other countries of diverse immigrants—Argentina, Australia, Brazil, Canada—did not develop commercial cultures possessed of the same versatility. Nor did the markets that fueled those commercial cultures become as integrated across geographical and social boundaries.

The new media and technologies also magnified the power of celebrities to participate in commercial culture. Whereas television began as a government-supported endeavor in many other countries, in the United States it was sponsored by companies whose products were lauded every hour by the stars on the screen. Hollywood became a factory for star salespeople, too, in contrast to the smaller film industries of Europe and Asia. John Wayne wanted you to smoke Camels, Lana Turner told you Max Factor's lipstick was the best, and Gene Kelly loved flying Air France. In the later years of the twentieth century, the relationships even began to work in reverse; sales-people from "Mikey" of Life cereal ("He likes it!") to Clara Peller of Wendy's ("Where's the beef?") were so universally recognized they became stars in their own right.

AMERICAN commercial culture has taken over the world, to the dismay of many, because it captures something that everyone seems to want: a dream life in which everyone is welcome, everyone can be rich, and everyone can be a star. The American ideal remains firmly ingrained in the minds of billions of people. You only had to see the global reaction to Barack Obama as he campaigned for and won the presidency. He represented the return, the renewal, and the confirmation of an ideal that had been damaged by George W. Bush. He was a handsome, camera-ready man with a picture-perfect family straight out of Hollywood's central casting, even if he needed a better stage name. He played basketball—the United States's most successful sporting export—drank bottled water, and even smoked a cigarette now and then. Above all, he sold. He sold the image, and he sold the dream.

Americans create that kind of image and that kind of dream better than anyone, and doing so helps them to sell just about everything. They have an excellent product pipeline, of course, but what would their top brands be without their starry endorsements and the massive publicity-advertising-marketing juggernauts that push them into the homes of people around the world?

Sure, other countries have advertising agencies, including some very successful ones. But they lack the authenticity of American campaigns, the pure American-ness that breaks down barriers and invades new markets in an almost naive way, much as Graham Greene's Quiet American foisted himself on Vietnam. Other countries have their own versions of Hollywood, too. Bollywood (in India) and Nollywood (in Nigeria) are far more prolific than Hollywood, but their stars, though increasing in recognition, can't match the pull of Hollywood royalty. With a very few exceptions, only American stars of television, movies, sports, and music have been able to dominate the entire world: Muhammad Ali, Marilyn Monroe, Madonna, Michael Jackson, Michael Jordan—and then Tiger Woods, Tom Cruise, and Hannah Montana. It stands to reason that the images of people like these would be good for selling things; sport and music transcend language and other differences, and action films—the United States still makes the most expensive and earth-shattering—do too. But from the rest of the world, can any stars compare to American stars in their iconic pull?

Roger Federer may be the only one. Soccer standouts like Cristiano Ronaldo, Lionel Messi, and Kaká have obtained huge contracts for endorsing athletic wear and personal care products, but they are largely unknown in the United States, which, with the European Union, is one of the world's two biggest export markets. The same goes for actors and singers who haven't been processed by the Hollywood and New York machines. Why is this the case? Quite simply, the blend of commercial culture and the enormous wealth of the United States can give its stars opportunities others simply don't have. For example, the corporate sponsors of snowboarder Shaun White, instantly recognizable by his mop of red hair, secretly built him a private half-pipe in rural Colorado so he could practice new tricks before the 2010 Olympic Winter Games in Vancouver. They knew it would be worthwhile; another victory for White, already an international star, would make their sponsorship even more valuable. At the games, he easily won his second straight gold medal.

Another advantage is cultural: English. The language is used in marketing campaigns around the world, even in countries where few locals speak it. Yet despite the dominance of English, many foreign stars fail to pick it up. Young soccer players drawn from around the world often spend years playing in Europe, even in England and Scotland, without learning the language. Many of them have grown up in poor countries where training takes precedence over education—unlike in the United States, where stars get private tutors and are encouraged to go to college. And plenty of foreign film stars, who may be models of poise on the big screen, even speaking carefully rehearsed lines in English, still stumble unconvincingly through interviews when they come to promote their work on American talk shows. A case in point was the appearance of Audrey Tautou, the star of *Amélie* and *The Da Vinci Code* on *The Late Late Show* with Craig Ferguson in September 2009. "I thought that, you know, I should have to wear a nice dress tonight so I can be silent, smile, you know?" she said. "That would be at least that, you know."

The English advantage is growing, too, as its speakers proliferate around the world. Though the populations of the major English-speaking countries are growing slowly, the spread of English as a second language is rapid and accelerating. There are probably about 500 million native speakers of English, but the total English speakers around the world may number 1.5 billion or more. This represents a gigantic market for the commercial-cultural combination that Americans will use to employ millions of people and to drive a vast part of their economy.

The Internet—an American invention—also presents an enormous boon to the economic nexus of commerce and culture. Until 2009, its entire architecture was built in English, or at least using the Roman alphabet. As a result, American culture became even easier to access, and harder to avoid. Platforms like YouTube have allowed plenty of ordinary people to become stars without Hollywood's help, but unless they speak English, they're better off sticking to the least common denominators that don't depend on language: music, slapstick, and cute little animals.

All of these factors only reinforce the power of the primary attribute that sits at the root of the American way of selling: its ability to transcend cultural differences by isolating the lowest common denominator. American businesses once used it to reach newly arrived communities in the young United States. Now they are using it as they ride the current wave of globalization to reach new markets overseas. No other country's salespeople are so accustomed to adapting and refining a sales pitch for new audiences.

BY this time, the American advantage in commercial-cultural activity should be clear enough. The question is, how will Americans exploit it to the fullest economic advantage? One way is to use it to sell more, to more people. The Internet is an obvious bridge into new markets, but those markets don't open automatically. For example, people in developing countries might want some of the American goods they see on the Internet, but if their customs systems are corrupt, bogged down in bureaucracy, or shot through with high tariffs, then they might not click "buy." To overcome this problem, the government of the United States will have to persuade other countries to make their import regimes more open and transparent. It has been trying for years, with only occasional success, through one-on-one trade negotiations and in larger forums like the World Trade Organization.

Americans can also go directly to new markets by opening branches of their businesses abroad. Sometimes they even try to give their most popular products a local spin. The fast-food chain McDonald's, for instance, briefly sold a sandwich called "Chicken McKorma" in the United Kingdom in an effort to attract customers in a market where Indian food, not Chinese food or pizza, is the take-out standard. But again, foreign governments can set limits on the scope of American companies' activities and on their ability to send profits back home.

There is a way to get around these limits: Americans could sell foreign brands to foreigners. If the supremacy of American commercial culture is to be believed, then an American sales-person could even help a Chinese automaker sell cars to the Chinese. Could this really happen? Absolutely. Americans might not be experts on foreign cultures, but the expertise culled from two centuries of pioneering a uniquely powerful way of selling could be the seasoning that makes the dish.

This opportunity will be especially great in countries that are just starting to build a modern consumer base. In just a couple of decades, China has created a middle class of about 300 million people. They don't have the buying power of a rich country's middle class, but they aren't poor, either. Americans will be able to help companies in emerging economies to culti-vate these consumers. They will also be able to help emerging economies' own brands find a global market, seeking out the lowest common denominator the way American brands have done so skillfully.

In the meantime, there will be other ways for the United States to export its unique expertise. It already exports its celeb-rities. Bill Murray famously dramatized this trend as a reluctant pitchman for Japanese whiskey in the film *Lost in Translation*, but the phenomenon is very real; for example, George Clooney has flashed his perfect smile for Nespresso, owned by Nestlé of Switzerland, for several years in advertisements across Europe, but not in the United States. The question is whether the United States will take the selling of celebrities to the next level, and actually start to produce them for export.

In fact, the American commercial-cultural machine is already doing exactly that, in a way that could only happen in the United States. It is harnessing the same diversity that gave it the commercial advantage to export its products and their cultural conveyances. Take the example of Masi Oka, who moved to the United States from Japan when he was a child and then became a star of the television series *Heroes*. In 2007, he was touring Asia with other cast members and even appearing on Japanese tele-vision shows, speaking in Japanese about his series, which, in its next season, featured a plotline set in Japan. Oka's ability to bridge markets clearly made him doubly valuable to NBC, the owner of the series.

There are bilingual stars in other countries, too, but they have had trouble making the leap in reverse, to American markets. American commercial culture sometimes incorporates influences from other lands, especially when those influences take root on American soil through its immigrant populations. But foreign stars, save for a few athletes and musicians, have had a much harder time making a dent in the American market. When foreign brands sell in the United States, they usually use American marketers and American faces. The trade in stars seems to be overwhelmingly one-way traffic. But could the United States become a re-exporter as well as an exporter?

In the trading of goods, re-exporters in one country receive products from suppliers in another country and then sell them to customers in a third country. Sometimes they add value to the products that they re-export by repackaging them or rejecting flawed items, but often they just take advantage of their commercial connections, their expertise in logistics, or the simple fact that their country has better transport options than the country that made the products. To do the same with stars, the United States would have to import them, process them somehow, and then export them, while making a profit along the way. One way to do this is to take budding stars from other countries, bring them to Hollywood, perfect their English if necessary, insert them into successful American cultural exports—television shows, movies, video games, etc.—and then send them back to their countries, and even third countries as well, to sell American brands. Actors like Penélope Cruz (*Vanilla Sky*) and Jean Reno (*The Professional*) got the treatment, as did English-speakers like Hugh Laurie (*House*) and Nicole Kidman (*Moulin Rouge*). By passing through the United States, they could become more famous in their own countries than if they had simply stayed and played the fame game at home.

Stars can bring in a lot of cash, and each of them can employ a fair number of handlers, helpers, agents, and marketers. But stars alone will not save the American worker; at the end of the day, they and their entourages are a small part of the labor force. Fortunately, what works for stars may also work for the less glamorous salespeople who make up the rank and file of the publicity, advertising, and marketing industries. Just as Hollywood trains and processes stars, the American commercial machine can exploit its edge by teaching other people how to sell—the American way.

Already, American business schools like the University of Pennsylvania's Wharton School and Carnegie Mellon's Tepper School are opening up branches in the Middle East, and others have gone to East Asia, like the University of Chicago. The University of Chicago has even opened a campus in London, competing head-to-head with the top European schools. But there may be an easier way to turn selling skills into exports: the same way tourism creates exports—on your own soil. Between 2003 and 2008, as the number of people employed in the American information technology industry grew three times as fast as the labor force as a whole, legions of foreign workers came to the United States to take jobs in the software, networking, and telecommunications industries. Many of them had obtained special, temporary permits intended for skilled workers—the famous and controversial H1-B visas—and many returned to their countries after their visas expired. If the sales industry is to grow as the Bureau of Labor Statistics predicts in the decades to come, why shouldn't foreigners come to the United States to learn how to sell?

FOR a set of skills that seems very abstract, based on a commercial culture that is hardly tangible, the American way of selling may generate a surprisingly large number of jobs, many with the potential to export. This is a reassuring possibility for a country that will depend more and more on the service sector to employ its people. For the possibility to become reality, Americans will have to perceive these opportunities and pursue them aggressively, acquiring the ancillary skills that they will need—foreign languages, for example—to capitalize on the skills they uniquely possess.

But the most important thing Americans can do to make sure that their advantage persists is to preserve the American ideal. When that ideal dies, as it almost did during the unpopular moments of the Bush administration's war on terror, people will no longer covet the American lifestyle and the products that go with it. They won't aspire to be like Americans if Americans are getting a bad rap around the world. Moreover, though Americans' skill at selling would still be a commodity, they themselves would be discredited and less sought out by foreigners. With the potential for millions of jobs to be created in sales and related fields, that risk is one the United States cannot afford to take.

Indeed, the welcome Americans receive in the rest of the world will be a crucial component of their economic opportunities in the years to come. As we'll see in the next chapter, the great sales force of the United States won't just sell to the world from their home base. Like Masi Oka, a star who bridges two cultures, the most versatile among them will go to the far corners of the world to sell American brands, and foreign brands as well.

7

AS THE GLOBAL ECONOMY INTEGRATES,
THE MIDDLEMAN WILL WIN.

One of the simplest and most important concepts in economics is that of gains from trade. When two people, two companies, or two countries produce goods and services, they can often benefit from trade with each other, thus taking advantage of differences in their skills and specialties. Opportunities to realize these gains from trade are among the most powerful ways for economies to move closer to fulfilling their potential. It's true that the creation of new products can create demand on its own—that's why we have the phrase "something you didn't know you needed"—but the most powerful way of generating new demand is by opening new markets and tapping legions of new consumers. If Nokia only manufactured and sold its mobile phones in its home country of Finland, with a population of just over five million people, the company would not have been worth almost $32 billion at the time of this writing.

To achieve gains from trade, the global economy is constantly growing and becoming more integrated through the processes we have come to know collectively as economic globalization. This economic globalization is not a new phenomenon. Though it is not necessarily steady or continuous, economic globalization has been the overall trend throughout recorded human history; with few exceptions, people around the world trade more now, and with more different partners, than they ever did before.

There have been setbacks, naturally. Starting at the dawn of the colonial period, political and ideological boundaries eventually closed down the caravan routes that had crisscrossed Europe, Asia, and North Africa. In the 1920s and 1930s, protectionism in the world's industrialized economies curtailed the sprawling growth in trade that had occurred since the turn of the century. And most recently the financial crisis of 2008 spurred protectionism again while taking the wind out of the global economy's sails.

The current wave of economic globalization is different from virtually all that came before, however. It has been driven primarily by the spread of information and technological advancements, rather than by exploration and political agreements. As we will see in the next chapter, political pacts can play an important role in helping economies to realize gains from trade. But even if the politicians don't cooperate, the overall trend across the decades and centuries has always been and will probably always be toward greater integration, simply because the gains from trade can be so large.

Within this context, who will be the big winners? One prediction that we often hear these days is that the middleman, the once unavoidable go-between for any sort of international trade, is going to fade away. Thomas Friedman, in his book *The World Is Flat*, argues that we must take action politically to make sure all the middlemen—part of the "fat" and "frictions" that he says slow the integration of the global economy—don't vanish altogether. Yet when you consider the economic forces in play, it seems more likely that the middleman will survive and even thrive with no trouble at all.

Consider the case of Alibaba.com, a fascinating and important company that Friedman neglects to mention in his book.

The Alibaba website calls itself "the world's largest online B2B marketplace"—in other words, a clearinghouse where buyers and sellers can get together to trade merchandise in bulk. It began in 1999 in Hangzhou, a picturesque and relatively wealthy city near Shanghai, as a way to connect English-speaking corporate buyers with suppliers of cheap manufactured goods in mainland China. Within three years, the business was profitable, and at the time of this writing, Alibaba had grown to connect 42 million registered users across 240 countries and regions. Its first stock sale, in 2007, was the biggest initial public offering since Google went public in 2004. The company is to international trade what eBay is to person-to-person commerce—and it is clearly nothing more than an online middleman.

The reason for Alibaba's success is simple: no one has the skills to do business in 240 countries and regions at once. Nor would you want anyone to have them; the effort required to study all those languages and do all that research would leave little time for the business at hand. When it comes to crossing borders to trade, middlemen are not just useful, they're often the efficient solution.

Indeed, middlemen can serve a variety of essential functions in the global economy. One is as simple intermediaries, putting individual buyers together with individual sellers the way Alibaba does. These relationships don't only occur between businesses, either. As globalization moves more people around the world, there will be more profits for relocation firms, which help economic migrants to settle into their new homes. There will also be more profits for the people who connect workers with employers: international recruitment agencies, outsourcing experts, and, lamentably, people smugglers.

Middlemen can also be the people who help to open entire markets. Companies expand abroad for many reasons: not just to find cheaper labor and new sources of raw materials, but also to open branches that do business with new groups of consumers. International investments can take many forms, and almost all of them require middlemen.

For example, take private equity funds. They raise money from big investors—pension funds, financial institutions, wealthy individuals, and others—and then buy companies, often in foreign countries. Usually, their goal is to take the companies they buy to the stock market, recouping their initial investments by selling shares to the public. Along with hedge funds, which buy companies at later stages, their cross-border purchases grew more than tenfold between 1987 and 2007. At every step, the funds require middlemen: analysts who identify the companies to buy, lawyers to deal with contractual issues in the funds' home countries and the countries of their targeted companies, and banks to underwrite the transactions, just to name a few.

It's no surprise that these middlemen's businesses have grown by leaps and bounds. Baker & McKenzie, which by various metrics has been the world's biggest law firm for more than twenty years, has been one of the prime beneficiaries. In 2009, its worldwide revenues topped $2 billion after four years in a row of double-digit growth. Those four years included three supposedly affected by the global downturn accompanying the financial crisis in the United States and Europe, but it didn't seem to affect Baker & McKenzie too much. Even in bad times, this middleman could keep winning, following the long-term trend underpinned by economic integration. The firm's services cater to individuals and companies trying to navigate the legal and regulatory frameworks of new markets, with practices devoted to trade and commerce, mergers and acquisitions, competition policy, financing, and tax law. And does Baker & McKenzie still have room to grow, even as some pundits say globalization is passing its peak? So far, the firm operates in thirty-nine countries—only about 150 more to go.

The idea that economic integration will make middlemen

better off is supported by some of the latest work in economic theory, too. Two of the world's top development economists, Pranab Bardhan of the University of California at Berkeley and Dilip Mookherjee of the London School of Economics, along with Masatoshi Tsumagari of Keio University, created a model that tries to capture the difficulties of international trade in a world like ours, where poor countries use relatively unskilled labor to produce goods that they sell to rich countries. In that world, a middleman can be necessary for two reasons. First, the producers in poor countries may simply be unable to sell directly to rich countries: think of farmers in Haiti, for example, who usually have only a small plot of land and may not even be able to write their own language. Second, the consumers in rich countries may insist on a high level of quality in the goods they buy, so someone must act as a filter for the exports coming out of the poor countries; an American consumer might not buy a bruised carrot that a Haitian consumer would think was perfectly edible.

In the academics' model, some fairly straightforward math shows that greater opening of markets will enrich the middlemen, even to the exclusion of the producers themselves. The producers don't have the bargaining power; the middlemen do. Freer trade also gives the rich countries an incentive to offshore more of the production of their own goods, which enriches the middlemen further. The basic result is clear: in much of the world, economic globalization should unlock more profits for the middleman.

Not only that, the middleman could end up standing alone as the winner in many countries. In theory, there are always gains from trade when markets open, and those gains can make people better off on both sides of the newly opened border. According to the model, however, middlemen can sop up the lion's share of the profit in poor countries, preventing the rank-and-file workers from getting rich. For the academics who created the model, this dynamic could help to explain why economic globalization hasn't reduced inequality very much in many poor countries.

THE examples above highlight what will probably happen in traditional industries like farming and textile manufacturing. But economies are not just made up of raw materials, machines, buildings, and the people who use them to make other goods and services. What binds these ingredients together are ideas: the how and why of each part of the productive process. When these ideas have owners, they're called intellectual property, and some industries use more intellectual property than others. Some industries, in fact, are made up almost entirely of intellectual property; they produce ideas in the form of books, movies, music, and software, as well as formulas and designs for other products.

These idea-intensive industries are becoming an ever-larger share of the global economy. They are concentrated in wealthy countries but are growing fast in the developing world as well. Even in its own backyard, Hollywood is now competing head-to-head with films made in Bollywood and Nollywood, mainly among immigrant audiences but occasionally in the mainstream, as with Mira Nair's *Monsoon Wedding* and Danny Boyle's *Slumdog Millionaire*. The same goes for software development, with companies from as far away as Siberia competing with the whiz kids in Silicon Valley. And virtually every idea-intensive industry has made the digital leap, transcending borders and using the Internet to develop, publicize, market, and sell its products.

One common conclusion about the idea-intensive economy is that it has cut out the middleman. Musicians now sell their music—when it's not being copied or pirated—directly to consumers. People sell used cars to one another without ever visiting a dealer. You can even buy cars online and pay with your credit card. The middleman looks as though he's disappearing, if he hasn't already.

Yet the opposite could and probably will happen. The middleman is here to stay, and it's likely that in many cases he'll get paid more than the producers of ideas themselves. But this time it won't be Colonel Tom booking gigs for Elvis. A new breed of middleman will arise, and those who ignore their services will do so at their peril.

Consider two of the biggest producers and processors of ideas on the planet: *The New York Times*, owned by the company of the same name, and CNN, which is owned by Time Warner, Inc. Every day, these two media outlets create billions of bits' worth of intellectual property: news stories and commentary, transmitted to the public as television, newspapers, websites, podcasts, e-mails, and even the occasional fax. Both of these companies are in a challenging industry at a difficult moment. News floods onto the Internet from around the world, often straight from the wire services, and no one wants to pay for any of it. Most of the budgets of the *Times* and CNN are paid for by advertising. But advertising isn't always a sure payday. Look at the website of the *Times*—the ads don't bring in as much cash as the ones in the printed newspaper used to, if people notice the ads at all. Watch a newscast of CNN International—it's filled with spots promoting CNN itself, not ads paid for by other companies.

In this climate, both companies will have needed to work hard to stretch the value of their products. The *Times* did so by trying to expand and create new products. It made television shows for a new channel. It bought websites that didn't carry news. It snapped up newspapers in other cities. It asked its reporters to appear on camera, to record downloadable interviews, and to connect directly to their readers.

All the while, though, the *Times* was just keeping its head above water. Despite getting into new businesses, using its expertise to manage other newspapers, and trying to stretch its people across new platforms, its income didn't rise fast enough to keep up with its burgeoning debt. At the time of this writing, its parent company's share price was down 86 percent from its peak in 2002.

Now consider CNN's strategy. Like the *Times*, CNN had news to sell. It had an international network of correspondents all feeding news back to its headquarters in Atlanta. And like the *Times*, CNN had started out on one platform—television—but had expanded to the Internet, where it was competing with the *Times* and other media companies. But instead of trying to bring the CNN magic to other television networks or branching out into new businesses, CNN stuck with the magic it had. The difference was that it found the right types of middlemen to bring its magic to more customers.

CNN had started out as an American company, bringing the news to Americans in their homes. It soon saw the opportunity to bring the same news to Americans traveling overseas, and indeed to any other English speakers who might care to watch. CNN began broadcasting the same programs it produced in Atlanta via satellite to the rest of the world. Soon enough, its executives figured out that people overseas might want a slightly different perspective from the American audience at home; CNN International was born, along with new headquarters in London and Hong Kong, staffed by English-speaking newscasters born in Britain, Australia, and even Argentina. So far, so good. But what was the next move?

After the first forays into the global arena, CNN realized that not everyone wanted the same news, though there was a lot of overlap in the news they did want. It also realized you only had to report the news once to get the story. But there was a missing link: how to get an English-language report into the eyes and ears of readers around the world. The middleman for CNN, clearly, would be the translator. Soon, CNN was offering its news in Arabic, Japanese, Korean, Spanish, and Turkish through dedicated television channels and websites.

Why didn't the *Times* spread its content in the same way, by hiring translators and launching websites loaded with advertisements in other languages? One reason was the underlying strategy that the *Times* has used for years: trying to identify people who could and, in the company's opinion, should be *Times* readers, and then convincing those people to buy the *Times*. For example, in 2008 the *Times* had about five million daily readers of the newspaper, but the company estimated there were as many as 80 million more potential readers in the United States alone. Those potential readers were the focus of costly advertising campaigns and changes in the newspaper's content. To pursue the international market, the *Times* took over the *International Herald Tribune* in 2003—it previously owned half of the newspaper—and later, in 2009, began offering an international version of the *Times*'s website in lieu of the *Herald Tribune*'s old site. But the dream remained to snap up all those typical *Times* readers who, for some reason, did not read the *Times*.

Was it the right dream? It's hard to believe that the majority of those potential readers did not know what the *Times* was or had never seen a copy of the newspaper or its website. More likely, they had gotten the chance to become regular *Times* readers and had turned it down. Yet the *Times* stuck with this strategy, missing out on the chance to use middlemen to expand its customer base. Now, you could argue that the articles in the *Times* are much more complex and involved than CNN's short news clips. But if the *Times* could hire the best journalists from around the world, couldn't it hire the best translators, too?

Meanwhile, as the *Times* limped along in a harsh environment for newspapers, CNN's profits rose sharply from 2004 onward. People from around the world could watch its newscasts and read its websites in their own languages, and millions did; the company still received a meager amount of revenue from each viewer, but it had multiplied its total audience without multiplying its costs. And though CNN has fallen on hard times lately, with ratings of its flagship American channel tumbling, CNN International has been profitable since its inception.

Translators are not the only middlemen, of course. In many industries, someone has to decide which products developed in one market will be tried out in other markets as well. One of the better-known successes in this category of middlemen is Roy Lee. Yet until *The New Yorker* profiled Lee in 2003, he was unknown to virtually everyone except the small cadre of film executives who formed his milieu. Lee's trade was to spot Asian films with compelling plots—mostly Japanese and Korean horror flicks—buy the rights to adapt the films for foreign markets, and then sell those rights to Hollywood studios. It was Lee, for example, who brought *The Ring* to the English-speaking world. What he did differed markedly from what translators did; whereas they transformed content to make it accessible in new markets at the behest of the companies that develop the content, Lee acted as a filter, spotting desirable content and helping to decide where it would be transformed and sold.

There are analogs to Lee in industries that deal with more tangible goods than news and film scripts. The clothing brand Lacoste is based in France, but it sells shirts, pants, jackets, shoes, and accessories with its famous alligator logo all over the world—with the help of some talented middlemen. Though most consumers don't know it, Lacoste does not sell exactly the same items of clothing in every market. In countries like Argentina, local designers are hired to shape and adjust the company's products for the local market. They use the designs that Lacoste develops in France as a template but have some freedom to infuse them with domestic tastes. Clearly, the company believes that the finishing touch middlemen provide makes the products that much more saleable.

In other cases, the middlemen work on the inside, in the home countries of the businesses trying to sell into foreign markets. At Haier, the Chinese electronics and appliances giant, a special research center investigates the cultures and needs of potential customers overseas so that the company's engineers can tailor their product lines accordingly; a single appliance might be sold in half a dozen slightly different designs.

Middlemen don't just transform products, either. They also act as fixers—the people who make it possible to do business in a place where the rules of the game are different from the rules in a company's home country. These are the lawyers, bankers, insurers, real estate agents, lobbyists, and other professionals who specialize in making foreigners at home in a new market. Naturally, they have to understand the rules in their clients' home countries just as well as they understand the rules in their own home countries so that they can communicate with their clients in a language that both sides understand. Because of the complexities of doing business abroad—just look at one of the World Bank's *Doing Business* reports if you want to see just how heterogeneous business practices and regulations can be—these gatekeepers are just as important as translators or product designers.

What kind of people will fit this description? Lee's case also demonstrates two important lessons about who the middlemen of the future will be. In an economic relationship that develops between two markets, the middleman could, in principle, come from either market as long as he is conversant in both. In rich countries, he is likely to be the child of immigrants from the other market, like Lee, or someone who has received a substantial education, probably at great cost, to become as knowledgeable about a specific market as someone like Lee. In poor countries, the middleman is likely to be a well-connected member of the elite—perhaps someone who received part of his or her education in the other market. And in both types of countries, it is possible that the middleman will be an emissary sent from a company in one market to work at a subsidiary in the other.

Whereas the rich country's middleman may well have worked his way up from humble beginnings in an immigrant family, the poor country's middleman is more probably someone who was already born into a high socioeconomic stratum. If these generalities hold true, then the shift of income toward the middlemen could lead to more inequality in poor countries, at the margin, and potentially less inequality in rich countries. But how quickly will the changes that could unleash these effects take place?

AS new markets open up in developing and industrialized countries, the products that the middlemen usher in—be they movies, polo shirts, or dishwashers—will have to compete head-to-head with locally manufactured counterparts as well as those from other exporters around the world. In all likelihood, the profits for any given exporter will follow a trend that is familiar to any first-year student of economics: they will start out positive, but as more producers enter the market and increase output, the profits will fall until there is little motivation for any further producers to enter. After that initial boon, the products will cease to be big earners for their producers, though they will continue to cover their costs.

This is why the middleman will win as the global economy continues to integrate. Every time a new market opens to trade, the middleman is the gatekeeper and as such will receive a share of the profits to be gained in that market. It doesn't matter if those profits eventually slacken; the middleman provides his service and receives his pay up front, since without him the profits available in that market would be zero.

In order to keep collecting that share, however, the middleman must be careful how he structures his business. Most middlemen must specialize in one country or region, since it's usually too difficult and time-consuming to acquire comprehensive knowledge of the laws, culture, or tastes of several very different places. Some middlemen, like Roy Lee, can also specialize in a single industry because of the specificity of their expertise or the complexity of the industry. That's all fine, as long as the middleman can serve more than one client. A middleman who specializes in one industry in one country for one client will see his value drop along with the company's profits, as explained above.

Because of these dynamics, the value of middlemen will depend strongly and directly on the speed with which new markets open. Their work will help to determine the pace and scale of trade, but they will be unable to do that work unless national leaders decide to open their borders to foreign goods and services. As we will discuss in the next chapter, the politicians may have to change course dramatically in order to keep the opportunities coming.

8

THE COLLAPSE OF THE WORLD TRADE ORGANIZATION WILL UNLOCK NEW GAINS FROM TRADE.

Middlemen can open markets one at a time, for one company at a time, but politicians can engineer much more sweeping changes. By agreeing on rules with their counterparts in other countries, they can open many markets at once to entire industries. The trade deals they cut with one another are often controversial—freer trade usually creates losers as well as winners, at least in the short term—but they can open up billions of dollars' worth of opportunities for economic growth.

Since 1995, most of the world's governments have pledged to work within a single international entity, the World Trade Organization, to open new markets for goods and services. During its life span, the WTO has been a repository of utter hatred or utopian hope, depending on your point of view. And the way things are going, it could end up being the shortest-lived of the international institutions set up to govern the global economy.

The WTO was founded as the main product of the so-called Uruguay Round of negotiations that dragged on for eight years before finally creating a basic framework for international trade. It replaced the General Agreement on Tariffs and Trade, a set of rules created by wealthy nations in the aftermath of

World War II, and its difficult birth presaged the problems that may lead to its demise.

The idea behind the WTO was noble enough. For the first time, even the smallest countries among the seventy-five initial members—from Antigua and Barbuda to Zambia—would have veto power over the regulations underlying global commerce. Every new decision would be made by consensus, including the admission of new members. Moreover, any member would be able to challenge any other member's practices through a system of courts officiated by impartial legal experts not affiliated with the parties in the dispute. When smaller members did not have the money or expertise to deal with new regulations or pursue disputes, the organization would offer training and assistance, paid for mostly by the bigger members, like the United States and the European Union. Together they would try to generate new economic opportunities by breaking down trade barriers in further rounds of talks.

So far, so good. But the WTO was only around for two years before it faced the first threat to its existence. At the 1997 meeting of trade ministers in Seattle, protestors assailed the conference site claiming that the WTO was biased against developing countries and that its opening of new markets was actually hurting workers more than helping them. The protests became a recurring feature of WTO meetings, even after the Doha Round was launched in 2001 with an explicit focus on the concerns of poorer nations. Soon, however, not only the people outside the security fences were protesting. Officials from developing countries walked out of the WTO's ministerial-level meeting in Cancún in 2003, disillusioned with the failure of their wealthier counterparts to follow through on the talks' supposed mandate.

By 2004, the "Quad" group (the United States, European Union, Canada, and Japan) that had previously sealed backroom deals to push negotiations forward had been replaced by the "Five Interested Parties" (the United States, European Union,

India, Brazil, and Australia). India and Brazil were supposed to represent the concerns of developing countries, and Australia's job was to lobby for countries more reliant on agriculture—the stickiest sector in the negotiations. Yet the failures continued, with another meeting ending in stalemate in Hong Kong in 2005 and the same result occurring again in Geneva in 2006. The members couldn't agree on some of the most fundamental issues: the subsidies that governments would be allowed to pay to their farmers, the openness of service industries to foreign businesses, and the timetables for imposing trade restrictions if imports were threatening to ruin domestic manufacturing sectors.

At this point, the protestors who continued to revile the WTO—notably the legions of Korean farmers who showed up to picket in Hong Kong—had become largely irrelevant. The negotiations were going nowhere. In fact, the ministerial meeting in Geneva that ended in December 2009 wasn't even slated to include official negotiating sessions. The WTO had failed in its mission to open markets, and it continued to operate mainly as a court system for trade disputes. In that area, wealthy countries had traditionally wielded a strong advantage. They had more money, more lawyers, more expertise, and more time to wage lengthy battles as each dispute moved from one ruling to another through seemingly endless sessions of committees and appellate boards.

It was not unusual for a dispute to drag on for years, or for the bigger members to have a dozen disputes open at the same time as both plaintiffs and defendants, often battling each other. A famous dispute about tariffs and quotas on banana exports pitted the United States against the European Union, with the United States joined by the Latin American countries that provided bananas to its importers, and the European Union joined by its former colonies. The dispute started in September 1995, the year of the WTO's founding, and it was the sixteenth case filed in the new body. It ended, after countless hours and dollars, in December 2009. By that time, 386 more disputes had been filed. In total, the United States was involved in 270 of the extant disputes as a complainant, respondent, or third party. The European Union was involved in 227.

This had begun to change, however, by the late 2000s. Poor countries were getting richer, and the assistance offered earlier by the WTO had begun to bear fruit. The smaller members of the group, perhaps feeling their power after derailing the plans of their wealthier counterparts in the Doha Round, started to call the bigger members on the carpet more often. They also started to win; for example, in 2007 the WTO found that the U.S. Commerce Department's treatment of imported shrimp contravened the group's rules after a complaint by Ecuador. The disputes the smaller members brought weren't necessarily that important in the general scheme of things; they might cost the big members a few million dollars' worth of legal services and potentially more in tariffs, as well as using up the valuable time of their officials. But, to paraphrase an old Washington chestnut: a million here, a million there, and pretty soon you're talking about real money.

Indeed, pretty soon the bigger, wealthier members of the WTO had to be asking themselves what the organization was good for. They wouldn't be using it to open any new markets for their countries' products if the Doha Round didn't go anywhere. The WTO had started out as a way to carry smaller countries along the path to a utopia of commerce, free of trade barriers and full of successful multinational businesses. It had turned into a monster.

And just like Frankenstein's monster, the WTO was doomed to die painfully and alone. The signs were already visible in the final years of the Doha Round, as the only one who seemed really eager to push the talks forward was the WTO's director-general, Pascal Lamy, a former trade commissioner of the European Union. He constantly exhorted the parties to sit down one more time at the bargaining table, to give up their sacred cows and make a deal. Yet the negotiators, even his former colleagues from Brussels, reacted only with reticence.

For one thing, they had already narrowed the scope of the talks so much that the economic benefit of any deal hardly seemed worth the fight. The World Bank estimated in 2006 that in the most likely scenario incomes in developing countries would rise by less than 0.3 percent net of inflation. The officials also risked suffering a political beating at the hands of whatever special interests they might harm if they signed a compromise deal. In the meantime, they had been having much better luck pursuing bilateral and regional trade agreements. During the first eight years of the Doha negotiations, the United States implemented one regional and eight bilateral trade agreements, while the European Union implemented ten bilateral deals.

Just shy of its fifteenth birthday in 2010, the WTO could already hear the faint sound of its death knell. The poor countries had dealt the heaviest blows as they tried to fight a system slanted against them, but the rich countries would be the ones to let the WTO die. The big question was, what would come next? Without an international body trying to break down trade barriers around the world, would all future gains from trade simply be left on the table?

THE answer will be no. Trade talks won't simply stop. Instead of taking place in a global, consensus-based system, however, they will happen only on a one-to-one or regional basis. By itself, this is no surprise; countries have negotiated bilateral and regional trade deals for decades. But as part of this process, the global economy will reorganize itself in a fascinating way.

The process will start with smaller, poorer countries: most of Africa, Latin America, and Central and Southeast Asia. Whereas big traders like the United States and the European

Union might be quite happy to negotiate outside of the WTO, these smaller and poorer countries will suddenly find themselves at an even deeper disadvantage. In the WTO, at least they had veto power over any agreement and, during negotiations, could choose to be represented by other, more powerful developing countries that often had similar interests. But left on their own, they will have to rely on the charity and self-interest of wealthy countries if they hope to improve their own access to overseas markets.

That charity often comes at a cost, and it's not always available to everyone. For example, the United States granted tariff-free imports to African countries under the African Growth and Opportunity Act, but only to the countries whose governments adhered to the American notion of democracy. Even then those countries still had to contend with so-called non-tariff barriers: rules about packing, storage, shipping, and documentation of goods that were often slanted against poor countries' exporters. The European Union, meanwhile, gave priority to its former colonies in Africa, the Caribbean, and the Pacific—too bad for extremely poor but excluded nations like Guatemala and Cambodia. In general, the big traders would only make concessions to these countries to cultivate them as strategic allies or if they saw special opportunities to exploit natural resources, the labor force, or consumer markets for their own businesses.

As a result of this lopsided situation, forming regional trade blocs will soon become a top priority for smaller, poorer countries. Banding together will be their only hope of improving their bargaining power in face-offs with the big three: the United States, the European Union, and China. And indeed, at the dawn of the twenty-first century, these blocs were already growing and becoming more economically integrated. The Association of Southeast Asian Nations (ASEAN), whose total output in 2008 was worth $1.5 trillion, was discussing the possibility of introducing a common currency at the time of this writing. Mercosur, the South American trading area anchored by Brazil, was in the process of inducting Venezuela as a new member and was talking with Central American countries about a free trade agreement as well. Africa continued to be stitched up in a crazy quilt of trade agreements, customs unions, and other economic alliances that offered little scope for negotiating with the major powers.

With time, these blocs will consolidate themselves, echoing the gigantic, continent-spanning economies predicted by George Orwell in his novel *1984*. But they won't necessarily be made up only of neighbors, like the European Union is now. Their membership will also follow the linkages engendered by the new colonialism. China may add adherents in Latin America and Africa, for example. The United States, which has been avidly pursuing a regional free trade agreement in the Middle East, may bring those faraway nations into its fold. These junior partners won't necessarily have an equal voice in negotiations between blocs, however. When it comes time to do a truly blockbuster deal, big trading powers like China and the United States may decide that the particulars are too important to be left to the little guys.

And there will be deals. These trading powers—be they individual countries or blocs—will inevitably begin to negotiate new trade agreements among themselves, as more-or-less equals. In fact, it is very likely that more markets will be opened through talks between five or six big powers than through a system like the WTO. Because the WTO is a consensus-based system, every agreement has to be approved by even the most stubborn members. There is no chance for members more willing to compromise to make deals among themselves, or to outvote the stalwarts. In the new setting, the two powers with the most common ground will be the first to make a deal to lower tariffs, reduce barriers against foreign firms entering domestic industries, relax import standards, or otherwise enhance trade. That deal, already, would represent more opening of markets than the WTO was able to achieve in the Doha Round. But the deal will have another very important effect: it will put pressure on all the other powers to sign deals with the first two, lest trade be diverted away from their own exporters.

This dynamic did not exist in the WTO. Stalwarts who blocked new trade agreements could be fairly sure they wouldn't suffer too many ill effects, because the WTO remained the main stage for opening markets. It was unlikely that a bilateral or regional agreement signed outside the WTO would make a significant dent in global trade flows. In the new setting, however, those bilateral and regional agreements will be the only game in town, a potential stage for blockbuster deals that outsiders will be helpless to block. Once one of those deals goes through, the pressure will be on every other trading power to catch up and restore the balance.

This leader-follower dynamic will become an important force in pushing forward international trade. Along the way, the resulting negotiations may have some very positive effects for the smaller countries, as their membership in blocs will bring them closer to the heart of the talks than they were in the WTO, with its more than 150 members. With time, they will pick up expertise and have a stronger voice within their blocs.

Of course, this dynamic will not always work; the stalwarts in the WTO will sometimes be the stalwarts in the new setting as well. As a result, global trade will become segmented, as it was during the Cold War. This time, however, the segmentation will occur along economic lines as well as political ones. The segments will still trade with one another—the WTO's old agreements won't just disappear—but their internal trade will be far more intense, turning even groups of geographically distant countries into coherent economic blocs. This will be unprecedented, and it will create opportunities lucrative enough to set a whole new set of economic dynamics in motion.

Take a simple example. Say that the world is composed of six trading powers: the United States, the European Union, China, Africa, Latin America, and the Rest of Asia. Trading norms are different in the two segments. In one segment—say the United States, China, and Africa—three powers trade with one another using tariffs lowered by agreements they have made among themselves. In the other segment—the European Union, Latin America, and the rest of Asia—the three remaining powers trade with one another using the higher tariffs specified under the old WTO's rules. The two segments are still free to trade with each other, but trade inside the first segment is intensified by the lower tariffs.

There are two important questions here. First, how much will global trade increase if the European Union's segment lowered its tariffs as well? The answer may be "not much," especially if the two segments are fairly similar to each other. With the United States, Africa, and China in the first segment, there will already be a lot of diversity in the goods and services this segment can produce, the types of workers it can employ, and the kinds of markets in which its transactions can take place. If the European Union's segment lowers its tariffs as well, then it may indeed take some business away from the first segment. But the total value of economic opportunities created—the gains from trade—may not change very much. After all, it won't matter much to an American clothing company whether its cheap garments are assembled in Nigeria or in Nicaragua, nor will a Chinese car company really care whether it sells its latest models in Baltimore or Berlin.

If, on the other hand, the segments are very different—say a "rich" one made up of the United States, the European Union, and China, and a "poor" one made up of Africa, Latin America, and the rest of Asia—then the lost economic opportunities will be much greater. Take the example of toy manufacturing, which usually uses cheap materials and low-wage workers. Toys coming into the rich segment from the poor segment will face higher tariffs than toys produced inside the rich segment. As a result, toy manufacturers in the rich segment will be able to pay higher wages to their workers and still match the prices of toys imported from the poor segment.

But there's a problem here. It doesn't make economic sense for workers in the rich segment, with their relatively high wages and productivity, to manufacture toys; they should be producing more advanced, higher-value goods. In other words, the rich segment would benefit from access to more cheap labor, just as the poor segment would benefit from access to more wealthy consumers. When the segments are different, passing up negotiations between them leaves a lot of the potential gains from trade on the table.

It's unlikely that the segments would form themselves along these rich-versus-poor lines, however, since the most difficult negotiations are usually the ones that take place between rich countries. In those talks—for example, between the United States and the European Union—opening the door to more exports doesn't necessarily mean lifting millions of people out of poverty; the parties are less desperate to open markets, and charity is no longer a motivation for concessions. Moreover, lowering trade barriers to another rich country filled with highly skilled workers can mean letting in the very imports that compete head-to-head with one's own companies' most valuable products.

So, let's go back to our original example of the two segments that are each fairly diverse: the United States-China-Africa segment and the European Union-Latin America-Rest of Asia segment. What will happen next? The two segments will continue their somewhat separate existences over the years, and the United States-China-Africa segment, with its lower internal tariffs, will benefit from more internal trade. Thanks to the extra trading activity, this segment will grow faster, and eventually it will open a gap with the European Union-Latin America-Rest of Asia segment; its material standards of living will, on average, be higher. Africans and Chinese will emerge from poverty faster than people from Latin America and the rest of Asia. Americans will get wealthier faster than Europeans. Now the two segments *will* be noticeably different. There will not be as many low-wage workers in the United States-China-Africa segment. The world will be in the rich-versus-poor situation, and, as in the toy manufacturing example above, there will be substantial gains from trade between the two segments.

At this point, with something worth talking about on the bargaining table, the members of the two segments may finally agree to sit down and talk. The gaps in incomes created by the segmented system may persuade the countries that were once obstacles to freer trade that they can wait no longer. That would be the most economically favorable scenario. Alternatively, the progress may not be enough to convince everyone to open their markets, and the world will again find itself in a stalemate. But along the way to that stalemate, many people's lives will have been improved. Many more of the gains from trade will have been realized than if the world had simply continued arguing in the meeting halls of the WTO.

This step-by-step process of negotiation may in fact actually lead back to something like the WTO. The old GATT could claim just eighteen countries by the end of 1948, its first year in existence. But by the time the Uruguay Round ended and the GATT was on the cusp of being replaced by the WTO, it had 128 members. If the segments do begin negotiating in earnest with one another—and there may be more segments, not just two— then they may find it useful to set up global trade talks again. Those talks aren't likely to mirror the WTO's current system, however. If the countries enter the system as segments, they will probably negotiate as segments as well. There will only be a few seats at the table, and the priorities advanced by the people in those seats will be determined as each segment chooses— perhaps by consensus, perhaps by majority voting, or perhaps by the preferences of the segment's dominant members.

If the world follows this path, abandoning the WTO may actually lead back to a system that opens markets for countries big and small. Despite the dirges of those who will mourn the WTO's passing, a shift to a world dominated—at least temporarily—by a few large trading powers could be a positive economic step for everyone. Almost everyone, that is.

THE world is made up of roughly two hundred countries, and quite a few are likely to be left out of the trading blocs. Even the WTO leaves about fifty countries out of its so-called global negotiations, though thirty can attend its meetings as observers. In the segmented system, some countries will be left out because they are too volatile politically; it's hard to negotiate with a country when the government might change several times from one year to the next. Others will be left out because, in the view of their wealthier counterparts, they are too poor or backward to offer anything useful—no natural resources, no millions of urban laborers ready to work in factories, no speakers of a common language to offer low-priced, outsourced services. Because many of these countries were never members of the WTO, its demise won't make much difference to them. But those that were members might feel like the first rung on a ladder to economic progress had just broken beneath their feet.

All of these neglected countries will have to fend for themselves in a world dominated by economic juggernauts, relying on aid and advice from groups like the United Nations Conference on Trade and Development to help them meet foreign standards for their exports. In the meantime, countries inside the blocs and segments will be benefiting from higher economic growth as a result of gains from trade. Just as important, they will experience the exchange of ideas that comes from day-to-day commerce and leads to innovation in the long term. With time, the left-out countries will fall further and further behind.

Next, one of two things will happen. If the gains from trade between the established blocs have been big enough, they may run into a shortage of low-wage workers. In that case, the blocs will probably become less finicky about their trading partners and start recruiting the poor countries that had previously been left out. (As any economist will point out, it doesn't matter if the wealthier countries are more efficient at producing every possible good or service; as long as their technology is slightly different from the poor countries' technology there will always be gains from trade between the two groups.) Countries that offer a combination of large populations and relative stability—such as Serbia and Ethiopia, which never became WTO members—will be the obvious candidates for the production of cheap manufactures and basic services.

But if the economies of the established trading blocs have changed substantially through the passage of time, then the opposite will be more likely to occur. Consumers' preferences may have changed enough so that they demand a totally different basket of goods and services. As the economic gap with the rejected countries widens, it will become more difficult for those countries to reverse course and join a bloc or segment. Quite simply, they will not be selling anything that the wealthier countries want to buy. In order to avoid complete exclusion from global trade, they will have to retool their economies to serve overseas markets.

Moreover, the segments are likely to become more and more integrated as their internal trade intensifies. The links between their members are unlikely to remain solely commercial: a common language may spread; they may institute a unified currency; joint ventures may collaborate on infrastructure projects like power generation; huge internal markets may develop for trading carbon emissions and other nontangible goods. The segments won't necessarily be as hermetically sealed as the old Soviet bloc, which had hundreds of billions of dollars' worth of internal trade each year, but they are likely to become progressively stricter when it comes to the criteria for accepting new members, just as the European Union has been in recent times. And without the WTO to stand in the way, the kinds of trade preferences that were once on their way out—import quotas, lower tariffs, and less stringent trading rules for favored countries—may make a comeback. Just as the European Union tried to favor its former colonies, the new colonialists (described in chapter 3) will likely try to favor theirs. The countries that missed the boat at the beginning of the post-WTO shakeout may find themselves standing on the pier for a very long time.

FOR the countries that do join the new global trading system, the question will be how much an expansion of trade will really benefit their people. Gains from trade can be converted into money pretty easily, but converting them into well-being takes another step. When trade increases, there are always winners and losers. In theory, you can spread those gains around enough to make everyone better off, but it doesn't happen automatically. This is one of the main reasons why trade talks were stalled in 2010: governments couldn't or wouldn't guarantee that their citizens would all be made better off by trade, so a broad range of groups, ranging from cash-rich industrial lobbies to grassroots movements representing millions of people, opposed any deal to open markets further.

And yet the distribution of the gains from trade will be a crucial determinant of the global economy's potential to grow, since gains concentrated in the hands of small elites rarely turn into long-lasting progress. For that to happen, broad sectors of the population need access to health care, education, and the wherewithal to start a business or invest in a new idea. This will be the big question mark in the future of global trade. The organization of the world into trading blocs and the onset of segmentation will support economic growth up to a point, but will the distribution of the gains from trade push it even further? In some countries, the answer will be yes. These countries will combine a variety of factors that created the incentive for, and even created a necessity for, effective systems for distributing the gains from trade.

The most important incentive driving this change will be the need to maximize the productivity of all an economy's workers, as discussed in the previous chapters. Some countries can grow even if they don't get the most out of all their workers. When competition from abroad means that some industries can't survive, like much of low-cost manufacturing in the West, these countries can simply sit back as the people who lose their jobs become dependent on social programs or settle for lower-paying, less-skilled positions in the labor market. The United States has adopted this attitude for decades, in the midst of steep drops in manufacturing employment. So has France, though in a different way; its culture of job security means that employed people are almost impossible to fire, but about 10 percent of the French workforce is permanently unemployed and completely unused in the French economy.

In the future, countries with aging populations, heavy obligations to pay pensions and medical costs for retired people, large public debts built up from years of budget deficits, and few easy sources of economic growth (for example, newly discovered petroleum reserves or rapidly improving technology) will be forced to act. They will need as many of their citizens as possible to work in as highly skilled jobs as possible, in order to collect more tax revenue and guarantee that living standards for everyone will keep rising.

Not every country in this situation will be able to make the change. To divert the gains from trade to government-led projects like scientific research, funding for innovative technologies that can spawn new industries, and retraining programs for displaced workers will require a somewhat progressive culture, despite the fact that pursuing these ideas will benefit all citizens. In addition, it will help if these countries can find a little extra money to jump-start these projects, though in the long term they will be financed by some sort of tax on the people who receive the biggest gains from trade: consumers who buy imported goods, shareholders and employees of businesses that benefit from open markets by exporting their products, and even small retailers who sell imported goods.

Under these criteria, the leading candidates to try to realize the economist's dream—expanding trade while redistributing the gains in a way that makes everyone better off—will be progressive countries with aging populations but relatively little debt. They will have the political bent needed to consider such a system (without dismissing it as socialism or some such nonsense) and the long-term budget position needed to pay the up-front cost of creating the system (without having to stretch their debts to the limit). Because of their aging populations, these countries will also feel the urgent imperative to get the most out of their current generations of workers.

To judge by today's conditions, the prime candidates to institute a system to redistribute the gains from international trade will be countries like Estonia, Slovenia, Australia, and Luxembourg. With the systems in place, these countries will also become the most likely to sign new trade agreements. For the first time ever, all of their own citizens—not just investors in particular sectors or workers in specific industries—will have nothing to fear and everything to gain from lowering tariffs and opening new markets. By laying the groundwork to take advantage of these new trading opportunities, these countries will turn the race to fulfill their economic potential from a long marathon into a flat-out sprint.

9

A NEW SET OF LIFESTYLE HUBS WILL REPLACE TODAY'S BUSINESS HUBS.

As we saw in the previous chapter, changes in trading rules will help to determine the new geography of the global economy. Some countries will have huge opportunities to grow through trade, while others will be stuck with contentious partners unwilling to deal. But some of the dynamics we have already discussed—the relaxing of migration rules and the rise of the middleman—will help create other opportunities that will cut across countries regardless of their positions in international trade: opportunities for cities to become economic hubs, drawing in slews of talented people and the money and resources that come with them.

With every major change in how the global economy works, a new set of economic hubs are created while others sink into irrelevance. It is a story that has been repeated many times before. Early on, there was Rome. Then, Damascus and Constantinople. Later, Venice, Antwerp, and London. New York and Hong Kong soon followed. Now Singapore and Dubai are waiting to step up to the podium. Traditionally, the hubs of the global economy have been centers of commerce: the capitals of empire, the crossroads of trading routes, financial powerhouses, and deepwater ports. Where the merchandise and money went, the people went as well. But that rule, which has held true for millennia, is finally changing. Now, people—not goods—will make the difference.

The first hints of change have come in the separation of financial markets from product markets. The biggest economic hubs—the biggest concentrations of money and economic might—are no longer manufacturing or even shipping hubs, they are financial hubs. The amounts of money that flow through them on a daily basis leave export centers and trans-shipment points looking puny. Today, when the discussion turns to the location of new economic hubs, that discussion depends heavily on the presence of the banks, law firms, markets, and concentrations of wealth that make financial hubs work.

As a result, the questions up to now have been mostly financial in nature: Will New York lose out to London because of currency and derivatives markets? Will Shanghai take over from Hong Kong, despite the fact that the powerful politicians from Shanghai who poured money into the city have disappeared from the top ranks in Beijing? Will Singapore and Dubai rise to the level of Tokyo, perhaps even superseding it? Will Brazil and India be able to create financial hubs of their own in São Paulo and Mumbai?

These questions assumed that the financial markets would change little over the coming decades. The questions also assumed that the markets would grow in the places that had the most cash. And finally, they assumed that the concept of a financial hub would still be meaningful many years into the future. All of these assumptions may turn out to be wrong.

Today's prognosticators look to China or Brazil as the future homes of financial hubs because of the vast pools of liquidity that are being accumulated in those countries through savings and foreign investment. Yet, as the recent financial crisis has shown, direct investments—purchases of stocks and bonds—are actually not the biggest part of financial markets. Derivatives are. So why would a major international bank, for example, trade derivatives in São Paulo? The derivatives market is completely global, and you don't need to have buyers or sellers who are based in Brazil to bet on the value of Brazilian companies, Brazilian government bonds, or even Brazilian weather and Brazilian crop prices.

Actually, you don't need to have buyers and sellers who are based anywhere in particular. More likely, the creation of new financial markets based in offshore tax havens, as we will see in the next chapter, will push the locus of financial power away from traditional centers and toward places where money doesn't physically live but can make a comfortable home electronically. Whereas some markets are moving offshore to new mini-hubs like Bermuda or Cyprus, the harmonization of financial regulations in the major economies (the United States, the European Union, and the United Kingdom) will make the choice of location within their borders less and less important. Why bother with trading floors in New York and London if the regulations are practically identical, and automated electronic trading is making working hours irrelevant?

Here's a better question: Why bother with trading floors at all? If the trading frauds exposed by the tumbling markets demonstrated anything, it was that having an employee physically present in the building of a financial institution was no protection against wrongdoing on a truly massive scale. In fact, it can even make wrongdoing easier. Consider the case of Nick Leeson, who bankrupted the British investment bank Barings through his illicit trading in 1995. Leeson was able to cover his tracks because he had physical access to all the crucial parts of the Barings operation where he was posted, in Singapore. He did the trading, and he could control the accounts by visiting the back office. Anyone could have figured out what he was doing if they had just focused on his trading and accounting patterns, but no one did until it was too late.

Clearly, the only things that can discourage and detect

huge frauds in the financial system are careful monitoring of the numbers—not the people—and strong incentives to play by the rules. Bernard Madoff was operating on Wall Street in plain sight for decades, even rising to the extremely visible position of chairman of the NASDAQ stock market, but anyone who had rigorously inspected his accounts (which the Securities and Exchange Commission never did) would have detected the pyramid scheme that cost his investors billions of dollars.

Given the advances in technology, there is no convincing reason to keep traders in close physical proximity. How many of them does a supervisor need to keep an eye on to manage his team? How many can he or she keep an eye on at the same time? Surely no more than the number who could easily be visible on a large computer screen, with live videoconferencing throughout the workday. If all the traders' files and data remain safely locked on the company's system, why shouldn't they work from wherever they want?

Well, how about because of the time difference? Even that argument will begin to fade. Trading of stocks, bonds, funds, derivatives, and currencies is becoming more and more electronic, so the sleeping hours of humans will be relevant to an ever-smaller share of the market. Moreover, within a reasonable time difference there are plenty of places people might rather live than in a traditional financial hub. Take Montevideo, which sits either one or two hours from New York, depending on the time of year, and three or four hours from London. It's a quiet, inexpensive coastal city lined with picturesque beaches and beautiful old buildings, and the food is great. Any trader living there and working over the Internet could adjust his or her working hours to be in sync with the bosses at the home office—that is, if the bosses were still there themselves.

THIS is the core of the new trend in economic hubs. They will not be hubs for trading merchandise, which have long been sliding out of the spotlight. They will not be financial hubs, either, because financial hubs will simply be unnecessary or too dispersed to be especially notable. Instead, they will be lifestyle hubs: places where people can live the lives they've imagined or even designed for themselves and still do their jobs, even if their companies are based thousands of miles away.

The new lifestyle hubs will be meritocratic places, in the sense that joining them will only require you to demonstrate economic self-sufficiency. People who can move—and changes in migration policies will allow more people to do so—will come from around the world, from rich countries and poor countries alike. They'll be entrepreneurs, investors, professionals, and even retirees. They'll all be looking for better places to live and work, leaving capital cities in developing countries where crime or climate are problematic, like São Paulo, Abuja, and Guatemala City. They'll also leave expensive cities with lousy weather, like London and Hong Kong, and those with high taxes, like Tokyo and New York.

Employers won't necessarily stand in the way of this trend, as they, too, will have much to gain. Middlemen will find their most productive locations as they straddle different cultures. The cost of living will be lower for them and for other workers, so there will be less pressure on their employers to raise their salaries. The workers will gain new perspectives and ideas about business by living in different environments. They'll probably be happier, too, which could make them more productive. And by giving workers the flexibility to move around while keeping the same job, companies will be able to maintain continuity in their workforces.

But who exactly will the workers in this group be, besides the middlemen? The people who move to the hubs will have several things in common: their jobs will be portable; they themselves will be mobile, with no family or other obligations anchoring them back home; and they will be seeking amenities that they cannot find—at least not at the same price—in their home cities. They will probably be highly skilled people working in occupations with nontangible products, since they will have to do their work via the Internet. They will be singles, couples, and young families; writers, programmers, designers, and engineers; some self-employed, most with university degrees, and all with a curiosity about the world beyond their home countries' borders.

So, which countries are candidates to host the new lifestyle hubs? A little analysis can reveal some interesting destinations. First, consider the attributes that mobile professionals will be seeking. They'll want to go to places where their money goes far, so the most expensive cities will be excluded. They'll also look for places where there's something for their money to buy, so it will be important that the locals have a decent standard of living, too; without that, there wouldn't be many interesting shops and restaurants around. Countries with a healthy respect for property rights will be more attractive, since the mobile professionals will probably want to own the homes where they live. They'll also want to go to places where the locals' human rights are respected, to avoid funneling hard currency to repressive regimes. And finally, the mobile professionals will likely avoid countries plagued by internal or external conflict; no one, except perhaps a few journalists and aid workers, wants to live in a war zone.

There are rough ways of measuring all these attributes. To see how far some hard currency would go, we can compare the value of a country's gross domestic product in dollars to its value in terms of local purchasing power. One hundred dollars buys a lot more stuff in Mexico than it does in the United States, so the purchasing power is higher south of the border. Mobile professionals looking for a kind of lifestyle arbitrage— obtaining a higher material standard of living in a new hub for the same money they spent in their former homes—will care a lot about that ratio.

To measure how well the locals are doing, there are many options. One of the most widely used is the United Nations' Human Development Index, which tries to measure human capacities through life expectancy, education levels, and local purchasing power. Adding respect for human rights to the equation, we might use the Global Human Rights Index prepared by a group of academics for the Green Party of England and Wales. Then, to figure out how much a country respects private property, we might try the International Property Rights Index, a measure of legal and political protections for individuals that is compiled by the Property Rights Alliance, a coalition of non-governmental organizations and think tanks. And finally, we could measure security and stability using the Global Peace Index from the Institute for Economics and Peace and the Economist Intelligence Unit.

A rough measure of the attractiveness of a country to mobile professionals might combine the purchasing power ratio, the Human Development Index, and the Global Peace Index, while ruling out countries with low ratings for human and property rights. By this measure, the top ten candidates to host a new lifestyle hub are Vietnam, the Czech Republic, Bulgaria, Malaysia, Singapore, Argentina, Slovenia, Costa Rica, Uruguay, and Tunisia. All of these are fairly peaceful, nonrepressive countries where the locals live pretty well, almost anyone can get a high-speed Internet connection, and a few thousand dollars a month can buy a very nice lifestyle. They're not necessarily commercial hubs now—only Singapore can claim to be any sort of economic center—but that's not the point. They offer an environment in which mobile professionals can do their work and enjoy life to the fullest.

For Americans and Western Europeans, some of these countries were hidden behind the Iron Curtain for decades. But tourists have been discovering the beauty of Prague and the dynamism of Ho Chi Minh City since the 1990s. Costa Rica and Argentina have become cut-rate playgrounds for millionaires and backpackers alike. Tunis and Kuala Lumpur are sophisticated cities in the Muslim world where non-Muslims also feel comfortable doing business.

These new lifestyle hubs will be existing cities that the international mobile workers decide to invade. The effects on local people could be severe. Local people could be priced out of their neighborhoods by foreigners bringing money from abroad to rent and buy housing. (This has already occurred in some neighborhoods of Buenos Aires, where prices have risen more than 100 percent in just a few years as foreigners, including the author, bought property there.) Foreigners will also drive up prices for other goods, since they have a greater ability to pay. Higher-priced restaurants and bars will open in their neighborhoods, pushing out more affordable places. Providers of services, from hairdressers to plumbers, will raise their prices to cater to the new market.

In addition, the foreigners will create their own subculture, and their lingua franca may not be the local language. In Dubai, which has been trying to market itself as a lifestyle hub for a decade, the high-income foreigners use English, not Arabic, to communicate, regardless of where they are from. They may not adhere to local customs, either. Drinking alcohol is prohibited by Islam, but foreigners imbibe freely in hotels, private clubs, and their own homes. Most local women in Dubai would never dream of wearing a bikini out in the open for fear that a man from outside their intimate circle might see them. Not so for foreign women, who lounge in minimal clothing on Dubai's hotel and country club beaches.

The overall impact of these tendencies—higher home prices, vendors preferring to serve wealthy foreigners, an expatriate subculture—will be to polarize and segregate the cities that become lifestyle hubs. Naturally, the situation will be more accentuated in cities that start from a lower base in terms of prices and incomes. The polarization and segregation will breed resentment among the local people, especially if they don't see many benefits from their new neighbors in the short term. But local governments won't do much to stop the trend; after all, these mobile professionals will be spending and investing hard currency in their districts. They'll be contributing tax revenue, too; even those who only pay income tax to the countries where their jobs are based will contribute, since they will be unable to avoid property taxes and some consumption-based taxes as well. And then there's the best part: as long as the local governments leave them to live as they please, they won't want anything to do with politics in their new homes. They'll be happy to live in blissful, polarized isolation, watching the news on television as though it were an entertaining sideshow, just as enclaves of foreigners already do in peaceful but less-than-democratic countries like the United Arab Emirates.

Such polarization won't be limited to existing cities that become lifestyle hubs. New cities are also being constructed from scratch to compete for the buying power, tax revenue, and prestige the mobile professionals can bring. For instance, investors in Bahrain (who may or may not include members of the island nation's monarchic government) are paying $2.5 billion to construct a mini-metropolis from scratch on the edge of the capital, Manama. The city, called Bahrain Bay, will be 60 percent residential—a clear indication it is meant for new arrivals in a small country whose population is already one-third foreign—and designed with luxury amenities and green technology. Bahrain is so intent on attracting foreigners that it contracted out the urban planning of the project; an architectural firm based in New York, not a committee of Bahraini officials, is essentially creating the city's zoning regulations on a case-by-case basis.

Many of the professionals who move to Bahrain Bay will do their jobs via the information superhighway, but they will hire other people to do everything else: clean their houses, wash their clothes, cook their meals, mind their children, and even, for the wealthiest among them, drive their cars and watch out for their personal security. These people will be poor locals—to be fair, there aren't many in Bahrain—or laborers imported especially for the purpose from poor countries nearby. To judge by the treatment of these people in places like Dubai and Hong Kong these days, they will receive a tiny room to live in, food to eat from the family table, and a salary that's just enough to cover the bare necessities and perhaps one trip home each year. And this situation is unlikely to change anytime soon, because the supply of these migrant workers, for the next decade at least, will seem almost infinite. They have virtually no bargaining power until they have worked successfully for several years in the same household; until then, any number of their peers could easily take their place.

Two classes will therefore develop in the newly constructed lifestyle hubs: the rich owners of property and the servants who attend to their daily needs. Some entrepreneurial locals may make a little money opening restaurants and shops to cater to the rich, but they'll have competition. Along with the professionals will undoubtedly arrive their favorite brands: restaurant chains purveying everything from the festive pig-outs of T.G.I. Friday's to the delicate Japanese-Peruvian creations of Nobu can already be found in several of the emerging lifestyle hubs. Luxury retailers like Louis Vuitton, Gucci, Prada, and Burberry are also strongly represented. The mobile professionals won't have to rely on local businesses; they'll bring their favorite businesses along with them.

SO, what will happen to the existing economic hubs? Some will simply disappear. Others may be able to transform themselves into lifestyle hubs. There are deep trends under way—shifts in liquidity, movements of businesses, and evolving political situations—that will determine how long that opportunity lasts.

In Singapore, for example, a wave of mobile professionals seeking a comfortable lifestyle may come just in time. At first glance, this tiny archipelago on the southern edge of Malaysia seems to have unlimited economic potential. Its government, which is essentially a one-party authoritarian regime, has created an entrepreneurial climate second to none; it is ranked by the World Bank as the easiest country in the world for doing business. It welcomes professionals from around the world as well as legions of migrant blue-collar workers. It has an excellent deepwater port and has become a nexus for petroleum trading and refining. Its location between India and China allows it to straddle two of the world's biggest emerging markets, and foreign companies doing deals in both of those countries routinely take advantage of Singapore's legal and financial frameworks to facilitate their transactions.

Despite its small size and lack of direct democratic rule, Singapore has managed to create a lucrative niche, garnering for itself a nice little percentage of the global economy's growth. That lucrative niche may soon disappear, however. Its attractiveness as an intermediary base for transactions in India and China will diminish as those countries allow more foreign law firms and investment banks to do business on their territory, and as they develop their own financial services sectors and legal frameworks. Already, India has lifted a ban on foreign investment banks and law firms working on its shores, though it continues to prevent foreign firms from actually practicing in its court system. And foreign firms looking for a foothold in Asia are going to Hong Kong, Beijing, and Shanghai rather than Singapore.

The petroleum market may also marginalize Singapore soon. Other countries in the region, from China to Cambodia, are planning to enhance their own refining capacity. Oil trading is becoming more virtual and more global, with after-hours and electronic trading making geography irrelevant, so Singapore's location as a bridge between the financial markets is less important every year. Even its port may lose significance as global warming opens the Northwest Passage through the Arctic. Trade involving Europe, Russia, China, and Japan will no longer have a reason to pass through Singapore's waters, as going through the Northwest Passage will save thousands of miles' worth of time and fuel.

Singapore's political model is also becoming less tenable, as migrant workers begin to demand the same rights as expatriate professionals and native Singaporeans. Even in a country where freedom of speech is limited, the migrants are protesting publicly as the weak global economy leaves them with less work, less income, and large debts. The deal that the Singaporean government has crafted with the residents of its territory— limited political freedom in exchange for unlimited economic freedom—is beginning to fray around the edges.

When these changes come to pass, Singapore will be left feeling a little bare, without some of the snazzy accoutrements that fueled decades of rapid growth. If it can maintain its attractiveness as a lifestyle hub, it may be able to reinvent itself and become a home to more mobile professionals. But they will be comparing other options—like temperate Sofia and historic Tunis—to a crowded, recently constructed city that sits right on the equator, with an average high temperature of 88 degrees Fahrenheit (31 degrees Celsius) and humidity over 70 percent. Singapore's population is aging steadily, and current projections suggest it will begin to shrink in 2030. As global warming worsens, Singapore won't just get hotter; rising oceans will also begin to rob it of the land that it reclaimed at significant cost from the waters that surround the main island. Becoming a lifestyle hub could be Singapore's only hope of avoiding a depressing decline, but it will have to compete with new entrants like Bahrain Bay to secure that future.

———————

THE mobile professionals' presence will be a boon for the local governments, a boon that will not go unnoticed by officials in other cities. Soon the beauty contest will begin, as cities attempt to nominate themselves as lifestyle hubs. They'll try to attract foreigners by offering them tax breaks and flexible visas. They may even bulldoze a few slums—places the locals would call neighborhoods—to build shiny new complexes of towering condominiums and green private parks, as cities from Phnom Penh to New Delhi have already done.

This won't be the easiest beauty contest to win, however. The mobile professionals' movements are likely to follow what economists would call an agglomeration pattern, or what sociologists might call a gravity model. In essence, the more people move to a place, the more pull they exert on similar people to come to the same place. There is an economic logic for this; if you believe that people interact with each other in productive and enjoyable ways, then the number of possible interactions may grow exponentially as the number of people in a group rises. On this basis, it's much more attractive to join a community of a thousand mobile professionals than it is to join a community of a hundred. Lifestyle hubs will have to reach a critical mass to start attracting significant numbers of mobile professionals.

Governing a lifestyle hub won't always be easy, either. The residents of the lifestyle hubs will not always have a voice in the political systems of the countries where they live, and their lives will be increasingly removed from their countries of origin. Some will raise children in their new homes, and those children will know little of their parents' culture. Many will give up their original citizenships to avoid paying taxes to governments whose services they no longer use.

Their position will pose a question faced by many immigrants and expatriates in the past: Is economic opportunity sufficient compensation for surrendering one's civil rights? And if not, who will represent these people? Unlike low-skilled economic migrants, these people will have the money to pay lawyers and lobbyists and to organize themselves if the deal offered by the lifestyle hubs ceases to be to their liking. This will be a very real possibility in places where the living standards of the locals fail to keep pace with those of their new neighbors.

To avoid this outcome, the new residents will have to learn to be good neighbors. Even though many of them will live in isolated communities—whether they start out segregated or just become that way by pricing locals out—they will have to reach out to the locals through altruism and social interaction to stop tensions before they start.

In this way, a new multinational polity is likely to form in the lifestyle hubs, a change that will also have distinct economic effects. Some mobile professionals will undoubtedly leave their long-distance jobs and start new businesses in partnership with the locals. This tendency will be particularly prevalent in hubs whose local economic cycles are out of sync with those of the mobile professionals' employers. The process of cooperation will lead to a merging of business cultures that may raise the local economy's long-term potential to grow, something that will be useful for countries hoping to diversify their industries. And some of the potential lifestyle hubs are starting to take notice. In 2009, for example, the government of Dubai began offering financial and technical assistance to expatriate entrepreneurs looking to start new businesses there.

THE mobile professionals' choice of where to live will have an impact on the rest of the world, too. The places they choose as hubs will quickly develop better transport and logistical links with major cities and exporting countries. If the routes to the new hubs become lucrative enough, they will start to pull traffic away from other nearby places. For example, if Ho Chi Minh City becomes a new hub, Vietnam Airlines will have a chance to take business away from Thailand's Thai Airways International, perhaps even replacing it on routes to the destinations preferred by the mobile professionals. Airlines in general stand to benefit from the expatriation of the mobile professionals, since they will undoubtedly want to fly home to see their bosses, friends, and extended families from time to time.

The news is less good for the governments of their countries of origin. They will be losing the buying power and tax revenue of thousands of highly compensated workers during the most productive periods of their lives. Supporting pensions and other publicly provided benefits will become more difficult. Prospects for the economic future in countries that already had trouble holding on to their most talented citizens will only worsen.

This brain drain will be the highest-value part of the massive shift in the world's human resources (discussed in chapter 4). Unlike that larger shift, it will have immediate adverse effects for rich and poor countries alike. They will all have to consider how best to hang on to their most likely emigrants, who will be among their most economically valuable citizens.

Some countries will undoubtedly resort to blunt measures, instituting rules about who can move abroad and who cannot. Yet when such rules were implemented in the past—for example, in the former Soviet Union and its satellites—they were routinely flouted by people hoping to emigrate, often with help from the countries hoping to welcome them. Enforcement of the rules sometimes involved threats of persecution against family members and friends who remained, which intensified the atmosphere of repression. If these tendencies recur in the future, they will likely lead to international isolation for the countries involved—a counterproductive result.

One more risk comes with the opportunities presented by the new lifestyle hubs. As discussed in the next chapter, some hubs may also become the centers of an enormous financial black market that is already beginning to form outside of the existing hubs. If that market suffers a crisis of the magnitude we saw in the traditional markets in 2008, the new hubs may disintegrate as quickly as they arose.

PART · IV

RISKS

10

AN ENORMOUS FINANCIAL BLACK MARKET WILL ARISE OUTSIDE OF TRADITIONAL CENTERS.

So far we have considered how the deep factors that underpin the world's economies can set the limits on their growth, the obstacles that can stand in the way of reaching those limits, and the opportunities that can speed the economies on their way to fulfilling their potential. We have focused on the challenges that individual countries will face because of their intrinsic characteristics and the choices those countries have made to date. But there are global challenges, too, that present risks to growth for the whole world. In 2008, the world came within a hair's breadth of tumbling into another Great Depression because of uncontrolled speculation, unchecked deception, and unrealistic expectations. The reaction to that crisis has set forces in motion that will fundamentally change the financial markets and possibly lead to more crises of equal peril.

To understand why, we have to rewind financial history. The last two decades witnessed the greatest expansion in financial markets the world has ever seen. At the heart of this expansion was the proliferation of derivatives. These are securities that are neither equity, like shares in a company, nor debt, like government bonds. Rather, they are gambles; their values are contingent on something the world does not yet know, like the future price of oil, whether a company will go bankrupt, or even the weather.

The emergence of derivatives was in some ways a great boon to humankind. Derivatives allowed people who wanted insurance to hedge and allowed people who thought they could predict the markets to speculate. Derivatives also gave individual investors and companies a plethora of options for controlling the level of risk in their portfolios. These new securities could truly make people better off, but they had to be used responsibly.

That did not always happen. Even if much of the derivatives market was useful and productive, enough of it was rotten to create the biggest financial crisis since the Great Depression. Once the world's financial authorities had injected enough money into the banking system and bailed out enough companies to put out the fire, they began looking for ways to avoid any future blazes. Naturally, they started by collecting ideas for new kinds of regulation—and not just any kind of regulation, but a monitoring and control framework that was right out of a science-fiction novel.

TAKE a step into the not too distant future. Imagine you're in a room filled with giant screens, keyboards, and consoles. Some of the screens show numbers, blinking and constantly changing. Others show maps that look like chains of constellations, solar systems, and even entire galaxies, with color-coded stars and planets forming clusters that expand and contract as if possessed by some invisible force. Suddenly, one of those clusters starts to explode in size, giving off a worrying glow and setting off alarms. The people watching the screens spring into action, barking the information into telephones and quickly arranging contingencies to stave off an imminent crisis.

Is this a view of an interstellar battle from the bridge of a spaceship, or perhaps the headquarters of a global nuclear power grid? No, but it might be the nerve center monitoring tomorrow's financial markets. The backward-looking, turn-a-blind-eye, too-little-too-late regulatory system that failed to fend off the current crisis is on its way out, a relic of the twentieth century.

Regulators around the world, often at the urging of American and British officials, allowed financial markets to spiral out of control during the 1990s and 2000s. Banks and other institutions took on unheard-of levels of leverage, making huge bets they would never be able to cover if the markets went south. Derivatives were their favorite tool, allowing them to speculate or hedge in ways that even the traders themselves sometimes failed to understand. On the flip side, consumers gamely took on enormous debts as the banks overextended themselves. It was a high-rise house of cards, and neither regulators nor executives asked too many questions about its foundations as long as the markets kept building it higher.

The alarm bells did sound, but it's easy to see why executives ignored them. The banks, hedge funds, and insurance companies that were taking on unprecedented leverage were also making unprecedented profits. No one wanted to hear dire predictions from the people charged with assessing risks, whether they were inside or outside the firm. Moreover, their calculations of risk usually showed that the financial institutions would be fine 99 percent of the time. Who would waste time worrying about that last 1 percent?

Meanwhile, the regulators suffered from equally profound problems. They weren't collecting the right information; for example, huge swaths of the market for derivatives, which allowed financial institutions to swap risks among themselves, went completely unobserved. Also, the regulators weren't collecting any information from enough institutions; trading by hedge funds and insurance companies was largely unmonitored.

To make matters worse, they were collecting a lot of information too late for it to be useful—quarterly instead of weekly or even daily. And they weren't using the information they did collect to draw the right conclusions, because their analysis often failed to consider the true worst-case scenarios. Even when they did, they didn't always have the power to do anything about it.

Not that the regulators weren't trying. For several years, financial institutions and regulators had been experimenting with ways to gauge what has come to be known as "systemic risk." Institutions like banks, insurance companies, and hedge funds were interested primarily in their own balance sheets. Regulators were interested in the stability of markets as a whole. While the private sector looked at individual risks, governments and international organizations like the Bank of International Settlements and the International Monetary Fund tried to gauge risks that would threaten the entire financial system. These systemic risks fell into two categories: risks to institutions that were too big to fail (because they would drag too many other players down with them), and risks to whole classes of institutions that followed similar strategies (because their individual decisions did not account for the effects of their herd behavior).

Regulators had a warning in the fall of 1998, when a little-known hedge fund called Long-Term Capital Management suddenly faced collapse over a series of bad bets on currencies and emerging economies' debt. It wouldn't have made news, except that earlier in the year the little fund from Connecticut had amassed 5 percent of the market where financial institutions traded risks with one another, based on securities with a value of about $1.25 trillion. In other words, LTCM was on the hook for roughly one out of every twenty dollars of the trades that banks, insurance companies, and hedge funds used to customize the risk profiles of their portfolios. The financial firms did this by paying one another to take on assets with uncertain returns, and their books were so finely balanced that a sudden 5 percent hole in the market had the potential to suck everyone else in. In Washington, the heads of the major financial regulators fired phone calls back and forth frantically until they finally arranged for a consortium of banks to bail out the fund.

What happened to LTCM should have alerted governments in the United States and elsewhere that the financial markets were slipping out of their regulatory grasp. Yet the authorities, even if they saw the writing on the wall, couldn't quite make out what it said. Two years later, the Commodities Futures Modernization Act removed whole categories of so-called over-the-counter derivatives from oversight in the United States. The idea was to remove any barriers to the expansion of the market, especially with strong competition coming from London as a center of financial innovation.

These over-the-counter derivatives weren't traded in any public market. Instead, they were made to order by banks and other firms for their clients; they could contain just about anything, and no one outside the transaction would be the wiser. Financial institutions traded these securities, both generic varieties and custom-made ones, without any regulator recording the transactions. Rather than learning the lesson of LTCM—that is, you shouldn't wait until it's too late to find out what's happening in derivatives markets—the government marched boldly in the opposite direction. Eight years later, it was in this over-the-counter trading that vast sums of credit-default swaps—bets on the viability of mortgage-backed securities— changed hands as the markets soared Icarus-like toward the heavens before tumbling down in flames.

Several more years passed and credit flowed freely thanks to the rock-bottom interest rates instituted by the world central banks in the wake of the American recession in 2001. But soon, an ominous cloud of never-before-seen leverage—people trading with money they didn't have—hung over the markets.

Debt levels for consumers, financial institutions, and even governments were higher than ever before. Many big banks were
holding assets and liabilities at least thirty times higher than
their net worth; it was the same as if you had borrowed enough
money to buy a $1,200 television with only $40 in your bank
account.

Finally, central banks around the world began trying out
new tools to identify systemic risks. They started by running
regular "stress tests" on the financial markets and encouraging
bigger banks to do the same. These tests were hypothetical
exercises in which researchers and risk managers would recal-
culate banks' balance sheets under seemingly extreme conditions: a doubling of benchmark interest rates, or an inability to
access short-term credit for thirty days. The problem was that
the stress tests only told part of the story: how individual institutions would suffer in extreme circumstances. But what if the
whole market was suffering? How would different firms interact if they were all facing the same stress at the same time?
How would they resolve all the trades and other connections
among them? The stress tests said nothing about what would
come next.

Recognizing the shortcomings of stress tests, the bankers
took the exercises a step further, with a tool called "crisis simu-
lation" or, more colloquially, "war games." Representatives of
different regulators and monetary authorities would huddle in
a room, or by teleconference or email, and act out emergency
scenarios the way Cold War generals had done only a few
decades earlier. A crisis would be presented: the failure of a
major bank or the collapse of the international network for
clearing payments between financial institutions. The officials
would react in real time, trying to overcome the crisis as their
own balance sheets went south.

The European Central Bank conducted two war games before
the current crisis. Researchers and officials from the bank sat

in different rooms, pretending to be the relevant authorities of several different countries and the ECB itself. They used a web-site to simulate and manage the crisis, and they spent a day stabilizing the world's financial system. They succeeded, but they had all the advantages. Everyone who needed to partici-pate was there—at least, people playing the appropriate roles were there—and they were all focused on the problem, all the time.

That's not what happens in real life. Financial crises can break out overnight, with little warning, and then last for months or years. But the war games were not just unrealistic; they were also incomplete in important ways. There was no participation from the commercial and investment banks, or the hedge funds that traded trillions of dollars in derivatives every day with the big banks, or the insurance companies that backed up the banks' bets. It was also very difficult, if not impossible, to simulate a crisis without knowing anything about the over-the-counter derivatives market. By the end of 2007, investors and financial institutions were using this market to cover the risks associated with almost $600 trillion worth of assets, often the same assets many times over. The value of the contracts themselves—the money that might actually change hands between the counterparties—was esti-mated at almost $15 trillion, an amount roughly equal to the value of all the goods and services the American economy produced in a year.

The authorities would need a much more detailed picture of the connections between financial institutions to prevent an event with unforeseen effects on the rest of the market, like the failure of Lehman Brothers in September 2008. That tear in the tightly knit fabric of the markets ended up unrav-eling in ways for which neither the banks (which lost billions overnight) nor governments (which scrambled to pick up the pieces, changing their plans several times) were sufficiently prepared. But how could they see that fabric for what it was, rather than just a collection of fraying individual threads?

RESEARCHERS and policymakers have proposed several solutions to the problem of systemic risk. Markus Brunnermeier, a professor at Princeton University, suggests a mathematical way to see if the markets are heading for a crisis. He begins with the data the Federal Reserve already collects. Every day, banks report a number to the Fed called value-at-risk. That number is the answer to a question like this one: "Over the next week, what is the most money you would expect to lose in 99 out of 100 cases?" Banks answer this question with mathematical models of their own risks, where the time period (in this case, a week) and the probability (1 in 100) are fixed. One week, the answer might be $100 million. The next week, if the markets are especially volatile, it might be $200 million.

The value-at-risk figures give the Fed a notion of how stable and secure the banks are, even if it is a notion calculated by the banks themselves. But when banks calculate their own value-at-risk, they can only guess how stable other banks are. As the crisis has made clear, the fortunes of one bank can easily affect others because of the trades and contracts that link them together. If one bank engages in risky behavior, it's not just putting itself at risk, just as smoking in a crowded restaurant doesn't just put your own lungs in danger.

This is where Brunnermeier had his insight: What if I knew the relationship between one bank's value-at-risk and the value-at-risk of the entire industry? Then I could see when a given bank was vulnerable to problems at other institutions, and I could tell that bank to make itself more secure. Moreover, I could see when herd behavior threatened to put a whole class of institutions in trouble. I would finally have a numerical measure of the kinds of spillover effects that almost allowed Lehman Brothers to drag all of Wall Street down with it.

Using data generated in the past—perhaps two decades' worth—banks could easily calculate the power of this relationship on a regular basis. Yet Brunnermeier observed that the relationship changed very slowly over time. To predict problems, he would have to use other information that was correlated with the onset of a dangerously strong relationship between conditions in the market and the fortunes of individual banks.

So far, a prime candidate is the degree of mismatch between the timing of banks' inflows and outflows of cash. These mismatches don't always show up on most balance sheets. But if a bank has to pay out a lot in the short term while waiting for cash to come in further down the road, chances are that it is in a vulnerable position.

In Brunnermeier's vision, not only banks but also hedge funds and insurance companies will report the value-at-risk relationship to the Fed on a daily or weekly basis. The data will have immediate implications for the firms' activities; if a number like the cash flow mismatch crosses a certain threshold, the firms will have to stop taking on new risks and stockpile more cash. If groups of firms start to show similar vulnerabilities, computers and human supervisors will see the pattern before it gets out of hand and will be able to warn their counterparts overseas, too. Small companies will not be exempted, because herd behavior among them can have just as powerful an effect as the misdeeds of a single big institution.

Even though Brunnermeier's solution requires collecting new data from thousands of firms, many of which currently report nothing to the Fed, some of his colleagues say his solution does not go far enough. They want to get more cosmic.

SAY the global financial system is the universe. Each financial center is a galaxy, a collection of stars, planets, and other celestial objects held close to one another by their own gravity, in this case the trades and contracts that tie them together. Some galaxies even touch each other—London and New York, for example—allowing gravitational forces to exert a powerful pull across them. Occasionally, an object gets pulled out of one galaxy and into another. If you could chart the entire universe and measure all the forces connecting every object inside it, you would have what economists and other scientists call a network map.

According to Andrew Lo, a professor of finance at the Massachusetts Institute of Technology, you can never fully understand what's going on in the markets until you can see that map. He doesn't want to rely on months-old statistics to see dangerous herd behavior or a financial institution becoming too big too fail. He wants to see it as it happens.

Lo says that it's not enough to look at just one measure or correlation. Rather, a regulator has to see the forest for the trees: an entire picture of the financial markets organized as a network map, where all the major financial institutions are represented by nodes and connected through their shared transactions. You can't just buy this map at your local service station or brokerage firm, however. All the financial institutions have to open their books and reveal their trading activity—not just amounts, but also counterparties and the structure of the transactions. Somehow, you have to gauge the risk inherent in those transactions, and how tightly they tie the institutions to their counterparties.

Lo realizes this is a tall task. But as a doctor famously said over the body of another science-fiction hero, the Six Million Dollar Man, "We have the technology." In his vision, a useful map would be updated daily through automated links to all the financial institutions big enough to feature on it. It would simply be a question of creating the interface.

And it is possible. At the Sandia National Laboratories in Albuquerque, New Mexico, government scientists working with the Federal Reserve and the European Central Bank have created network maps of the world's biggest payments systems: the exchanges run by the Fed and the ECB through which banks conduct transactions among themselves. The Fed's system alone is home to $2 trillion in transactions per day. So at any one moment some nodes in those maps are extremely congested; they signify banks that are involved in transactions with many other institutions. Others have just a couple of connections to other nodes. In the Sandia model, the connections between the nodes don't yet show how deep those connections are. At the very least, a regulator can observe whether a given node is becoming much more important in a short period of time. And if a crisis is already under way, a regulator can see how the various policy options—like letting Lehman Brothers fail—might play out.

SO far, policymakers are taking seriously the idea of a new, invasive monitoring system for financial institutions. In the United States, Representative Barney Frank, the chairman of the House Financial Services Committee, said in late 2009 that he thought Lo's ideas showed a lot of potential. But the most telling sign came earlier that year, when the leaders of the European Union decided they needed a plan to compete with American proposals for the future of financial regulation. They turned to Jacques de Larosière, one of the most experienced international bankers on the continent. He had run the International Monetary Fund for almost a decade, had spent five years each at the helms of the French central bank and the European Bank for Reconstruction and Development, and was a top advisor to the French Treasury and BNP Paribas, the huge French bank. De Larosière came back with an eighty-six-page report on how to fix financial regulation. He wanted an agency to monitor systemic risk, and he wanted maps.

Buried deep in the report is Section 242, which reads as follows:

> A comprehensive early warning system could also usefully be complemented by the creation of an international risk map and an international credit register. The purpose of such a risk map would be to build up a common data base containing relevant information on risk exposures of financial institutions and markets, both at the national and the international level. The risk map should contain all the information needed for identifying systemic risks on a global scale. Clearly, in order to be effective, the risk map should go beyond the banking sector and include major other financial institutions like insurance companies and hedge funds. It should also include all major financial products. Subject to suitable rules for protecting confidentiality of firm-level data, such a risk map would close the information gap revealed in the current crisis and could become an essential tool for everybody interested in assessing risks to financial stability.

The paragraph might as well have come straight out of the testimony Lo had given before Congress in 2008. The de Larosière report was endorsed heartily by newspapers across Europe, including the influential *Financial Times*, and became the main document of reference for the European Union's regulatory reform efforts, driven forward by the ambitious French president, Nicolas Sarkozy.

Thus, in the early months of 2009, legislators and functionaries around the world—but mostly in the main centers of financial power: Washington (Congress and the Fed), Frankfurt (the ECB), Brussels (the European Union), and London (Parliament and the Bank of England)—were working feverishly to come up with a regulatory scheme to which the governments of all the major economies could agree. In the march toward high-tech, forward-looking, global regulation, the time for blue-ribbon reports and research papers had ended; the time for consensus and compromise had begun.

Yet when the leaders of the G-20, the group of the world's biggest economies and a few other regional powers, met in London in April 2009, the talk was more of short-term economic stimulus than of new financial regulation. In his public comments, the meeting's host, British prime minister Gordon Brown, singled out tax havens for special attention, saying that "the old tax havens have no place in this new world."

Tax havens? It wasn't too surprising. The enormous stimulus packages that Brown and his counterparts hastily enacted in the midst of the global recession were set to threaten their governments' bottom lines for years to come. Collecting more tax was one way to close the gap, and cracking down on tax havens seemed like a relatively efficient way to do it. In fact, tax havens were becoming a huge headache for all of the major economies, as companies moved their corporate headquarters to low-tax Bermuda and high-earning individuals relocated their homes to low-tax Switzerland.

Shortly after the meeting, the Organization for Economic Cooperation and Development—another club of rich countries—named and shamed four countries who had yet to comply with its rules discouraging tax avoidance: Costa Rica, Malaysia, the Philippines, and Uruguay. Within days they, too, had agreed to comply with international standards for reporting the incomes of expatriates. But the rich countries were fighting last year's battle. They should have been more worried about financial havens—escapes from regulation as a whole, rather than escapes from mere taxation.

FINANCIAL havens? Well, why not? The new, science-fiction-style regulatory scheme—even if only one or two of the main financial powers adopted it—would inevitably take three things away from traders of derivatives and other securities: privacy, freedom, and money. Privacy, because hedge funds and other entities that had never been required to discuss their balance sheets or their trading strategies with regulators would suddenly have to open up; moreover, big trades in derivatives used to balance risk—the kinds of trades most banks and funds like to keep secret so their competitors won't know where they're hoping to make money—would have to take place on an exchange. Freedom, because regulators were barring the trading of some kinds of securities and some trading strategies, like short-selling a sharply declining stock or betting on mortgage defaults without holding any of the mortgages in question; in addition, firms would no longer be able to trade custom-made securities as quickly as they could develop them, because the securities would have to be approved by the regulators first. And money, because complying with the regulations would require firms to install systems for reporting trades and hire people to staff them, and because the loss of privacy and freedom would make some lines of business evaporate. Financial firms couldn't make millions using derivatives to help Enron and Greece hide their debts—as Wall Street's banks did in 2001 and 2009—if everyone else, including the regulators, knew exactly what they were doing every step of the way.

You could argue that limiting all of these things is regulation's job: to slow down a market that could go out of control during its most profitable moment. But there will always be people who want to push the envelope, who want to take that extra bit of risk, even if the government says it's a bad idea. In the financial markets, these people aren't drunken teenagers seeing how fast their parents' station wagons can go. They're often smart, innovative thinkers used to finding ways around complex problems. They will also have help.

It's very unlikely that every single country in the world will cooperate with the new financial regulatory regime. That's because the new wave of financial regulation will amount to a sort of cartel. All the cartel's members will try to maintain an economic framework that may hurt them all individually but should help them all collectively. But cartels always have the same problem: the incentive to rebel is huge, and it grows as the rules of the cartel become stricter.

In the Organization of the Petroleum Exporting Countries, probably the most famous cartel, each country caps its own oil production so that, as a group, they keep prices high. Every member, however, has the incentive to sell a little more oil than its quota, turning a quick profit but making the rest of the members suffer as prices fall. In the new regulatory setup, there is a similar trade-off: a little less business in the financial industry, in return for a lower probability of another economically disastrous crisis.

Naturally, the conceivers of the new regulatory regime would like to see compliance from every country in the world that is home to a big financial institution. Yet the incentive, especially for a small country, is to opt out. If you thought the Cayman Islands was notorious as a tax haven, imagine what it could be like as a financial haven: huge skyscrapers filled with currency and derivatives traders reliving the go-go days of New York, London, and Hong Kong, when they and their bonuses ruled the world.

This is already happening. Just consider what Derek Adler, the director of Ifina, a firm that administers investment funds in the British Virgin Islands, had to say in a report published by the industry magazine *Hedgeweek* in November 2009: "Investors in offshore funds are typically institutions and high net-worth individuals that are big enough and experienced enough to look after themselves. They don't need the heavily regulated products that are typically set up onshore but prefer offshore products with a lighter regulatory touch. Finally, as a

consequence of these factors, the expertise and sophistica-
tion of local service providers tends to perpetuate the use of
offshore vehicles." In other words, rich people and financial
institutions are trying to escape stringent rules in traditional
centers by going offshore, and, once they go offshore, they
stay.

The British Virgin Islands have some regulations of their own,
but the rules are nowhere near as strict as those in the United
States, the United Kingdom, or the European Union. Other
financial havens are even looser. As of this writing, the International Monetary Fund had labeled twenty-six countries and
territories, from Andorra to Vanuatu, as "offshore financial centers." A report on the British Virgin Islands published in 2004
stated that the territory had "most of the essential elements for
a suitable framework for financial supervision." A similar report
on the nearby Turks and Caicos Islands found "numerous gaps"
in financial monitoring, including "inadequate powers for the
supervisors to carry out their responsibilities."

As this offshore migration of sophisticated investors continues, these smaller financial centers will provide the backbone for an enormous, parallel financial market—a financial
black market, trading mostly over the Internet but based in a
constellation of would-be tax havens and other small countries. New banks will spring up, competing with their counterparts in the major economies by staying off the radar, using all
the forbidden tools and operating with lower costs. As the
trading volume in the black market grows, the incentive for
older financial institutions to join it will grow as well, through
offshore subsidiaries or "special purpose vehicles" of the kind
made famous by Enron's accounting statements. For the older
institutions, the alternative will be to sit by and watch as their
customers leave the regulated market to take advantage of the
lower costs, greater privacy, and broader trading freedom in
the financial havens. Indeed, several of them already have
branches in offshore centers, like Canada's Scotiabank in the

Turks and Caicos Islands and Britain's Barclays in the British Virgin Islands.

Many of the banks that do business in the black market won't just be dipping their toes in, either. As long as they maintain their operations in the regulated world, they will still have to report their trades; the black market banks may not even want to do business with them. Pulling up stakes in the traditional financial centers and moving all operations to the black market will be the only way to take advantage of those tempting benefits and hang on to those customers.

Some financial institutions will remain in the regulated world, of course, to deal with day-to-day needs that aren't easily imported, like home mortgages, car insurance, and credit cards. But the real big-money stuff—the billions upon billions of dollars in daily trading that top banks, funds, and insurance companies used to reap huge profits during the last two decades—will go offshore. There are already plenty of financial institutions based outside of the major markets; the Cayman Islands is home to about 10,000 hedge funds, the same as the United States. They will just have to move all their trading offshore, too.

Will it really be possible to move all this trading offshore, even if the assets are onshore? Sure—all a trader needs to know is if the assets exist, and how much they're worth. In fact, some of these offshore markets already exist. You can take bets on the value of stock market indexes, or the likelihood that an American automaker will go out of business, on the gambling websites already located in many of the same places regarded as tax havens or offshore centers today.

Outlandish as it may seem, these websites are already trading a kind of derivative: synthetic securities, which mimic the behavior of real stocks and bonds without having any link to the underlying assets. At the time of this writing you could log onto the website of 32Red, an online casino based in Gibraltar, and see links for "Online Casino," "Poker," "Bingo," and "Spread

Betting." Selecting "Spread Betting" would take you to an affiliated website where you could bet on the future values of thousands of stocks, stock indexes, commodities, Treasury bonds, and currencies—all without holding any of the underlying securities. It is just like betting on the weather or the outcome of a sports contest.

The amazing thing is that these little websites are providing exactly the same service as many derivatives markets. If you want to protect yourself against the risks of your investments in stocks or bonds, you don't have to buy options or futures anymore; you just have to place a bet that acts like a hedge against changes in their value. During the recent economic crisis, an Irish website called Intrade offered bets on whether American automakers would file for bankruptcy. A holder of General Motors bonds, for example, could insure himself against a default by betting that the company would go under; if he was right, he'd recoup some of the money he lost when the company failed to repay all of its debts. By offering these bets, the Intrade website essentially turned itself into an exchange for "credit derivatives," a category that includes the "credit default swaps" whose misguided usage helped cause the recent crisis.

Nothing makes the parallel clearer—trillions of dollars of trades in the financial markets are simply gambling, not investing. Traders bet on how a number will change from one day to the next without ever owning something—a stock, a bond, or a mortgage—that has intrinsic value or a claim on an asset. Of course, the financial types have come up with a fancier name for this practice; they call it "naked" trading. The practice is completely unregulated—again, it has long been seen as a legitimate and useful part of the market for risk—though politicians and regulators have been talking seriously about forcing traders to put some clothes on, at least at the major financial institutions.

Because the gambling websites already offer users naked trading, they are poised to become the black market trading floors of the future. But the financial black market, swimming in the same excesses that doomed the booms of the 1990s and 2000s, will inevitably crash under its own momentum as well—most likely the first time clients need to take out their money, in other words, when the next global economic crisis hits. With the world's big economies ever more synchronized, such a crisis may come sooner rather than later, perhaps less than ten years after the financial black market reaches maturity.

At that point, the investors and companies that have moved to the financial black market may find themselves falling without a net. After all, this market arose in a grab bag of self-styled financial centers: island nations that began as tax havens, small countries looking for a new source of tax revenue, and emerging economies trying to punch above their weight. These countries won't be able to rescue failing banks and bail out investors the way the established financial powers did in 2008 and 2009. They simply won't be able to raise the necessary amounts of money; their tax bases are too small, and they'll probably have a hard time borrowing money from the regulated market.

The regulated market will be fairly insulated from any *direct* consequences of such a crisis, as long as it manages to make sure the remaining financial institutions aren't dabbling in the black market. Some governments in the regulated market may bail out individual investors, the way the United Kingdom bailed out its citizens after they lost their savings in Icelandic banks in 2008, but they will have to be careful of setting a precedent that will lead to more risky behavior in the future. More likely, a crisis in the financial black market will leave investors with virtually no protection against a total collapse.

As a result, a crisis in the financial black market will have serious *indirect* consequences for the regulated market; after all, many independent investors will probably have money in both, and they'll have to pull money out of the regulated market to cover their losses in the black market. A rash of asset sales will ensue, pulling down stock and bond prices in the regulated market and sending interest rates skyward. Even with institutions insulated from the financial black market, the regulated market will still suffer the contagious economic effects of the crisis.

Also, in the aftermath of the crisis in the financial black market, some bankers and traders will undoubtedly flee back to the regulated world, creating a surplus of financial workers, pulling down wages, and raising unemployment while the market is in retreat. Those prodigal sons and daughters won't find the same world they left years before. The new regime will have created peculiar incentives for the financial institutions that stayed, too.

REGULATORS usually draw bright lines when they decide to monitor a new class of financial institutions. They don't want to impose unnecessary burdens on small businesses, and they usually don't have the resources to monitor every single institution in the class. Take those 10,000 hedge funds in the United States; a monitoring system based on a network map could display some basic information about them, but understanding their trading strategies in detail would require the staff at a regulatory agency to give each fund some personal attention—attention that might not seem merited if the fund was too small to threaten the entire market.

Indeed, according to officials in the European Union, it's likely that regulators will want to keep tabs on the biggest fifty or hundred actors in a given class: banks, insurance companies, hedge funds, and other big investors. So there will be a strong incentive for big institutions—especially those on the cusp of falling under supervision—to make themselves smaller. The atomization of banks, funds, and insurance companies that will result won't necessarily make the markets safer, though.

Rather, it will make the kind of herd behavior that accelerated the recent crisis even more difficult to curb, for the simple reason that more actors mean more possible herds.

They'll also find new ways to avoid regulation. For example, two banks interested in balancing their risks might decide to found a joint venture. Inside the new business, traders from the two banks would engage in the kind of risk-swapping they used to do without any sort of supervision in the over-the-counter market. But instead of more money changing hands, the value of the two banks' shares in the venture would change according to the success of their trading strategies. They might start out by investing $100 million each. If one bank got the better of the other in, say, a bet on the future path of short-term interest rates at the Bank of England, then they might settle the matter by valuing the first bank's share at $105 million and the second bank's share at $95 million.

Meanwhile, even after its first crisis, the financial black market will not simply disappear. A new generation of traders will always be willing to take the place of the last. If the long line of crashes since the dawn of the modern markets tells us anything, it is that greed and the appetite for risk always outpace the prerogatives of security and safety. After all, that's why we have casinos. But does that mean the task of regulating the financial markets is hopeless?

Not entirely. Even if these predictions come true, the regulators will have taken a step toward one important goal: isolating the average household from the worst effects of a financial crisis and thus preventing the next financial crisis from turning into an economic one.

The reason comes from a tendency that the financial black market is unlikely to change. Despite the flourishing of millions of investment options around the world, most people still invest the bulk of their money in their home markets. The overall share of money invested at home has gone down slightly in the past couple of decades, but the tendency is still very strong in places like the United States, the European Union, Japan, and now China. If regulation drives the most voracious speculation offshore, the markets that remain in the major economies will be smaller and poorer. But they may also become less volatile and populated by more transparent trading entities—banks and funds without the huge leverage, infinite subsidiaries, and "special purpose vehicles" that have recently plagued the markets—which will make them safer for the average investor, too.

This is not to say the old markets will become immune to crises under the new regulatory regime. Undoubtedly, they will again run into trouble for the same reasons they always have: smart people continuing to innovate beyond the reach of regulation, and nervous people continuing to trade on waves of hysteria. But the new crises probably will not be as deep, or as frequent, as they otherwise may have been.

The average investor will have a clearly delineated choice: play it safe in the regulated market or give in to greed and take a chance in the financial black market. A chance, because it's very likely that crises will happen in the black market more frequently than they did even in the unregulated version of the traditional market. That's because the black market will attract the most speculative investors and the most exotic, intricate transactions, while much of the safe money will stay in the regulated world.

Yet because individual investors can put money wherever they want, the two markets will never be completely separate. Authorities in the regulated market (the Americans, the British, and the Europeans) may bar their own people from investing in the black market, but they will still be left with foreign participants (the Chinese, the Saudis, and everyone else) who straddle both markets. To ban the foreigners from the regulated market would be to give up a huge amount of liquidity and trading.

With many investors still straddling both markets, a crisis

in the black market—and we should certainly expect a serious one—will still be able to cause havoc in the regulated market. As a result, the black market will pose a risk to the entire financial system. It will be up to the authorities in the regulated market to monitor this risk and try to minimize it by sealing their market off as much as possible. For the regulated market, further separation from the black market will be the only path to safety.

11

GLOBAL WARMING WILL MAKE RICH COUNTRIES CLEANER AND RICHER AND POOR COUNTRIES DIRTIER AND POORER.

The second important risk facing the global economy, climate change, is just as surely a by-product of integration and growth as the ballooning of the financial markets. The opening of new markets has allowed the world's economic output to rise by more than 150 percent since 1980, and pollution has grown apace. A broad scientific consensus now confirms that this pollution is raising the ambient temperature in many parts of the world, on land and in the water. It is a slow-moving trend, but its economic effects will resonate just as profoundly as the lightning strikes of the financial crisis.

More than a decade ago, the economist Jeffrey Sachs pointed out that one of the main factors determining the fate of nations was climate. Most of the world's poor countries are in the hot zones between the Tropics of Cancer and Capricorn, and most of the rich ones are in the temperate bands outside those latitudes. From an economic perspective, heat brings a variety of problems. It dries up water and makes growing crops more difficult. It takes the energy out of workers who can take only so much sun each day. It fosters large populations of insects that can spread disease; there's no annual frost to kill them off. It even helps microorganisms to reproduce, causing food to rot and helping infections to spread.

Dealing with heat is also expensive. To make water drinkable and move it around, a country may need desalinization plants and irrigation lines. It may even have to buy water from other countries if it doesn't have enough of its own. To make sure workers stay cool and productive, its businesses need buildings that provide shade and air conditioning. To keep them healthy, its public health system must invest in vaccines and sanitation. And a hot country has to hope that its neighbors are doing these things, too, so the heat doesn't make them irritable and potentially threatening.

With such costly challenges to overcome just to climb past the bottom rungs on the economic ladder, it's no surprise that hot countries tend to be poor. What will happen when they get hotter?

Baseline predictions of global warming estimate that temperatures in the world's tropical regions will rise by several degrees Celsius over the coming century, with the biggest changes occurring in Saharan Africa and Amazonia. Other poor regions, like Central Asia and southern Africa, will also be strongly affected. The Intergovernmental Panel on Climate Change, the winner of the Nobel Peace Prize along with Al Gore, has predicted that by the 2050s as many as 800 million people in Africa—almost 40 percent of the continent's projected population—will have difficulties finding enough water for daily needs. The panel also warned that because 80 percent of Africans rely on biomass for fuel, the continent's already tenuous energy security may also be at risk. In Latin America, the panel found a strong relationship between the spread of epidemics and changes in temperature and weather patterns. And in Asia, as many as 132 million people may be added to the number at risk of hunger by 2050.

Even if the panel's estimates are off by half—the numbers

have become a source of controversy since they were released—
the overall forecast is still frightening. Life will become even
harder for countries that, by and large, are already poor. They
will be desperate to find ways to raise their living standards in
the midst of rising temperatures. Succumbing to the new colonialism will inevitably be one way. Another will have to do
with the very methods imposed to stop global warming.

For decades, first-year economics students have learned about
something called "tradeable pollution rights" in classes that
deal with market failures. Pollution has clear costs to society; it
fouls the air we breathe and leads to climate change. Cleaning
up or preventing pollution costs money, too. These costs are
measurable, yet market forces don't choose the amount of pollution that society as a whole would choose. That's because the
causes of pollution depend on decisions by individuals and
businesses—whether to drive a car, how much steel to produce—
rather than decisions made by society. You don't usually con-
sult all your neighbors and take their preferences into account
when you buy a car. If you did, you might buy a compact
hatchback instead of a sport-utility vehicle.

The market needs help when it comes to controlling pollution, but it's not an easy problem to solve. Society should try
to reduce pollution in the least costly way, but who can constantly compare the costs of prevention and cleanup in every
business and household? This is where economists see a different role for the market. Imagine that society could set a cap on
the total amount of pollution each year, for example, the number of tons of carbon dioxide, sulfur dioxide, and other gases
emitted into the atmosphere. Then it could take that cap and
divvy it up as "pollution rights" among businesses and consumers. The total quantity of "pollution rights" would equal
the cap for the year, and any polluter that polluted more than
its rights allowed would be severely penalized. But polluters
would be allowed to trade the rights among themselves, at
whatever prices they saw fit. Polluters who could easily avoid

pollution would sell their rights to polluters who had a harder time cutting down; the latter group would be willing to pay as long as the cost was less than the cost of actually reducing pollution. Every year, the market would figure out the most efficient way for society to keep pollution under the cap.

Sounds ingenious, right? It certainly does, and that's one reason why there is powerful support—including from President Barack Obama—for instituting a cap-and-trade system at the global level, to replace the targets set by the Kyoto Protocol and other climate-related agreements. But there are two big problems with international cap-and-trade. The first is easy to see: who decides which countries get the biggest quantities of pollution rights? The second, hinted at two decades ago by Lawrence H. Summers, one of Obama's top economic advisors, is that the system may make poor countries much, much dirtier.

THE allocation of pollution rights is a momentous decision, because cutting pollution is such an expensive business. New technologies are being developed all the time to do the job: scrubbers that remove harmful gases from smokestacks, carbon sequestration devices that bottle up the gases and store them, designer bacteria that eat the gases and turn them into less harmful ones, and even wilder stuff than that. Then there are the alternative energy sources, those that don't burn fossil fuels to create electric power: wind, sun, geothermal, nuclear, hydroelectric. And finally, there are new fuels: biodiesel, ethanol, hydrogen, vegetable oil, you name it. Switching over to any of these technologies costs money, and very often that cost is the same wherever you are in the world. Not everyone has the same ability to pay, however.

In poor countries everywhere, millions of crude cylinders of charcoal are used every day for cooking. They are immensely polluting, but it is virtually impossible to replace them with a cleaner technology. Their users aren't connected to electric grids, so clean-power generators are out. Charcoal made from wood is the cheapest widely available substance with high energy output, so alternative fuels are unfeasible. Until these people have more money, they will have to pollute. And the same pattern is repeated with their transportation (seen any hybrid mopeds lately?) and in their factories, whose budgets are minuscule compared to those of their counterparts in rich countries. Few businesses in poor countries can afford to buy high-tech scrubbers or install wind turbines on their roofs. What they do have is a lot of cheap labor, but most technologies created to fight pollution don't depend on people power. They tend to be developed in rich countries and, like most industries in rich countries, use a lot of capital rather than a lot of labor.

So if cutting pollution is too expensive, what's the alternative? Under a cap-and-trade system, the only other choice would be to buy pollution rights from other countries. That, too, will be expensive for poor countries, since wealthier countries will probably bid up the prices. Poor countries will be caught in a bind, with living standards falling as their economies shoulder the burden of costly cuts to pollution, costly purchases of pollution rights, or some combination of the two. Their only chance of succor will be if the organizers of the cap-and-trade system deign to give them a lot of pollution rights.

On a global basis, most poor countries don't pollute very much. Most of their people don't own cars, which create more greenhouse gases than any other consumer goods, and they can't afford to buy the tons of throwaway manufactured items that rich consumers take for granted, like plastic water bottles and disposable diapers. Some of their governments have even argued that they have a right to pollute as they industrialize, just as the rich countries did at the same stage in their economic development. Yet most proposals for cap-and-trade systems would give no country enough pollution rights to maintain its current levels of emissions, so that all countries—at least in principle—would have an incentive to cut back.

If poor countries do receive generous allowances of pollution rights, it's less likely they will reduce pollution substantially. After all, they won't have to. And there will also be another, more subtle effect. The price of pollution in poor countries will essentially drop, and multinational corporations may decide to relocate their most polluting activities to the poor countries, hoping to get a nice, big share of the polluting pie.

A similar situation was foreseen in 1991 by Summers, then the chief economist of the World Bank and, more recently, director of the National Economic Council in the Obama administration. In a memo that was leaked to *The Economist*, Summers suggested that poor countries were underpolluted. Waste disposal was so expensive in rich countries, he reasoned, that they should ship their garbage to poor countries, who would gladly accept it along with cash payments. The problem is that poor countries are often exploited in these arrangements (as when companies from rich countries break laws by shipping toxic waste), and sometimes they do a poor job of managing the garbage once it reaches their shores (as when the local governments are too corrupt or have regulatory frameworks that are too weak to protect their citizens).

With all of these forces in play, there are three possible outcomes under a cap-and-trade system. First, poor countries may receive paltry allowances of pollution rights, in which case the burden of cutting pollution or buying more rights will make them poorer still. Second, if poor countries do indeed receive generous allowances of pollution rights, they will become more polluted. Or, most likely, some combination of the first two outcomes will result: a bit poorer, and a bit dirtier.

In the meantime, rich countries will continue to profit from the development of green technologies. Their governments have the money to make massive investments in basic research that will, very probably, lead to useful innovations and new products to be sold around the world. In fact, the United States and the European Union have adopted the green banner as the standard for future gains in the productivity of their labor forces, just as the Internet was in the 1990s. Some developing countries have tried to jump on the bandwagon as well, like India with its leadership in wind power, but it's hard to imagine a small, poor country like Laos or Honduras mounting the same kind of effort.

Still, there is one potential saving grace for poor countries: carbon credits. Cleaning up pollution is expensive, and so is preventing it, but doing other things to offset it isn't always so costly. These days, people who buy airline tickets on a well-traveled route like New York to London can pay a little extra to plant some trees, the idea being that the carbon-dioxide-absorbing power of the trees will offset the nasty emissions created by the transatlantic flight. Those trees aren't usually planted in the United States or the United Kingdom, however. Generally, the airline or travel agent contracts with a tree-planting company in a country where planting trees is easy and inexpensive, like Brazil. The business of creating carbon credits takes advantage of the one thing poor countries' economies can always offer: a copious supply of cheap labor.

This is exactly what poor countries need to turn this chapter's prediction on its head. People in rich countries can pay them to do something that actually reduces greenhouse gases, making the poor countries richer and their air cleaner. The problem is, it may not actually work. There are plenty of questions about exactly how much carbon dioxide can be absorbed by trees, whether trees are actually the best way to eliminate the gas, how verifiable the actions of carbon-offsetting companies are, and if carbon offsets can actually make a meaningful dent in emissions.

And beyond all of those doubts, there is the possibility that offsetting pollution with physical and biological mechanisms that absorb carbon dioxide may also be worse for the planet— that is, less effective in reducing global warming—than simply reducing pollution. If this is true, then carbon credits may be counterproductive, especially if they end up selling cheaply because so many countries want to supply them, as some experts have warned. Either way, carbon credits can only solve one part of the pollution problem. Trees and other plants may eat up carbon dioxide, but they don't do much for emissions of carbon monoxide, sulfur dioxide, nitrous oxide, mercury, and other harmful emissions; a cap-and-trade system could set separate pollution rights for each of those substances.

AS poor countries become poorer and dirtier, they will begin to suffer other problems as well. Clean water will be harder to come by. Crops will suffer from perennial droughts. The heat will make productive work more difficult. And, since most poor countries have birth rates far higher than those in the wealthier parts of the world, their populations will balloon even as their lands become less livable. With more people but no appreciable increase in resources, living standards will fall even further. As privation takes its toll, conflict will likely result. Old grudges will become pretexts for wars fought to control water, food, and fuel. Poor countries will begin to slip backward not just economically but socially as well.

When this begins to happen and poor countries are having tremendous difficulties providing basic services and ensuring affordable food and water supplies for their people, the colonizers discussed in chapter 3 will see an opportunity. They'll be able to buy up vast swaths of land on the cheap, because of the reduced yields caused by global warming and the pressure felt by the local governments. The massive economies of scale that can be gained with modern agricultural techniques will make farming the land worthwhile for the colonizers, and perhaps other multinational operators as well, even if it isn't for smallholders.

The land will be less populated, since subsistence farming will have become harder to sustain and the temptation to migrate will have intensified. But China can send legions of its own low-wage workers to farm, and Saudi Arabia can bring in thousands of low-wage workers from other countries, as it did to build its cities and do the grunt work on its oil installations. Thus global warming will intensify the colonization wave, pushing local people off their land and making way for the mega-farms needed to feed the world's fast-growing economies.

We have already discussed the problems with new colonial arrangements, and the deals that result from global warming are likely to be even worse. The gap between the high-tech farms run by the colonizers and the subsistence plots that surround them will be stark. As locals have a harder time feeding their families, they will see thousands of tons of food being exported to feed people in countries thousands of miles away. Yet their governments will have a hard time resisting the offer of the colonizers: millions and perhaps billions of dollars in up-front cash to stop, or at least slow, a downward spiral of poverty.

This trend will worry foreign governments, too. In addition to worsening local tensions, it will allow the colonizers to expand their spheres of influence more rapidly than ever. The colonizers don't necessarily want to create military bases around the world, but they do have foreign policy agendas that their colonies' local governments will feel compelled to support. And, of course, the people who emigrate from lands made unlivable by global warming will be seeking new homes in more temperate climes. Yet they won't necessarily be the migrants that the wealthier countries want, as we saw in chapter 4. So how can the rest of the world stop global warming from unleashing these destabilizing dynamics?

A first step would be to try to mitigate the factors that exacerbate the effects of global warming. The changes in temperature are not huge—just a few degrees over the course of the next several decades—but man-made problems like pollution, deforestation, and poor water management can turn them into major challenges. Fast-growing developing countries have repeatedly shown an unwillingness to control pollution as assiduously as the governments of wealthy countries would like; they argue that the wealthy countries had a chance to industrialize without that constraint, and they should as well. Deforestation, which has been blamed for landslides, droughts, floods, and even for worsening global warming (since trees absorb carbon dioxide), is also a common problem in developing countries from Haiti to Malawi. The governments of these countries often lack the capacity—and sometimes the will—to stop poor people from chopping down trees in remote rural areas, and they may also be susceptible to bribes from logging companies seeking new sources of lumber. Water management is also especially tricky in developing countries, since the legal and physical infrastructures needed to keep water clean and distribute it equitably are often missing. Global warming and these harmful practices are likely to reinforce each other, creating a vicious circle. If people are under pressure—perhaps even at risk of going hungry—then their governments are likely to focus on their short-term needs and ignore the long-term damage their actions may cause.

Wealthy countries can help with all of these problems, and they may find it in their interest to do so. Rather than sending checks or issuing loans to developing countries, they could provide in-kind aid, not as money but in the form of useful goods and services: scrubbers for smokestacks, building materials and cooking fuels to substitute for lumber, and purification systems for water. Indeed, one can see a potential global deal forming between rich and poor countries. The poor countries would have to control their pollution as the rich countries have argued they should, so that the problem of global warming does not get worse. But in return for participating in an effort to cut emissions, the rich countries would provide the poor countries with enough in-kind aid to make a meaningful improvement in their overall environmental-economic situations.

Even if the political consensus needed to achieve this deal can be achieved, there may still be regions of the world in which the fight against global warming seems to be a losing battle. In some regions of India, according to estimates by William Cline of the Center for Global Development, crop yields may drop by almost half if global warming is not curtailed by the 2080s. In Africa, already-dry countries like Senegal and Sudan will see similar reductions. And the world food supply as a whole could also shrink, despite the beneficial effect of warming on areas closer to the earth's poles.

Were these changes to occur, the discussion about how to deal with global warming could center on a new question: whether some regions of the planet should be inhabited at all. Lower crop yields will result in food security problems and lower export revenues for poor countries, and their ability to help people stuck in increasingly arid areas will be limited. Rich countries, even those that might have signed up to help poor countries adapt to global warming, may decide it is simply not worth trying to make these dry regions artificially habitable.

When the battle is conceded, the residents of these regions will have to find a new place to live. Most likely, they will move to their countries' cities; indeed, this is already occurring. If the countries have a reasonable business climate and can attract foreign investment, the sudden appearance of millions of low-wage workers could create an enormous opportunity. Local and foreign companies would be able to open new factories producing low-cost manufactures for export, a step that is often the first one along the path to lasting economic development. (As seen in chapter 1, a rural-to-urban migration can provide the labor force for a decades-long growth spurt.) Alternatively, if the affected countries cannot attract investment money, then the newly arrived internal migrants may find themselves living in slums far from home with no work or other means of support. Their inevitable restlessness would likely lead to instability, an extra problem for governments that would already be under significant pressure from lower tax revenues and expanding demand for social services.

If wealthy countries perceive this risk, they may feel compelled to do something about it. Instability in poor countries tends to create problems for rich countries, too: prices for commodities produced in the unstable countries may zoom higher; the foreign operations of rich countries' corporations may be interrupted; trading and shipping routes may be blocked; insurance rates may rise; disillusioned locals may become violent and strike at their perceived foreign enemies, both locally and abroad. To fend off these risks, rich countries may try to help the displaced people by creating jobs locally, despite the lack of a welcoming business climate. Or they may prefer to allow "climate change refugees," as Sachs has called them, to migrate to their own shores, as political refugees have done for years. There will be a sort of historical justice in either of these courses of action, since it has been the advanced countries' pollution produced over decades of industrial growth, and not just the pollution produced by developing countries in recent years that has led to global warming. But justice won't be their most pressing reason to take action; protecting their own interests will.

SO far, action has been limited and even misdirected. In November 2009, Gordon Brown, then the British prime minister, and Nicolas Sarkozy, the French president, announced plans for a $10 billion fund to help poor countries fight global warming. Half of the money, according to Brown, would be used to help them cut their own emissions; the other half would go toward what was arguably a much more pressing need: helping them deal with the toll that the emissions from every country in the world would be taking on their people.

Indeed, the bigger question here is whether the world as a whole will do something to prevent global warming from worsening. At the heart of this question is a classic "tragedy of the commons"—everyone lives on the same planet, yet no one has sufficient incentive on their own to cut pollution, since an individual effort is expensive and unlikely to be pivotal. As the problems of developing countries spill over into rich countries, their incentives will become increasingly aligned. This will happen because global warming is likely to become more costly as it progresses. For every degree temperatures rise, the economic problems that global warming creates will be exacerbated, even if its direct effects on the climate remain steady.

The reason has to do with the way people are affected by changes at the margins of their lives. If you begin taking food away from them, for example, the first kilogram of rice doesn't hurt as much as the fifth; as you take more away, people are pushed closer to a bare level of subsistence, and it's harder for them to keep substituting other foods for staples. Similarly, the first thousand people who move from the country into a city probably have an easier time finding jobs and places to live than the tenth thousand. And the more temperatures rise, the more costly it will be to fight global warming and reverse these trends; most companies will have started by using the cheapest ways to reduce pollution and, as they are asked to reduce it further will have to resort to more expensive methods.

Now, there will certainly be a temptation for businesses in rich and poor countries alike to take advantage of the increasing tensions that global warming will produce. If cutting emissions becomes more valuable—that is, if the damage caused by pollution becomes progressively more serious, then the companies that supply emissions-reducing technologies will make enormous profits, since their own cost of production probably won't increase as quickly. They won't necessarily argue against an international climate control consensus, since it may be in their interest. But food prices will also rise sharply if global warming affects the supply of staple crops enough to cause shortages, resulting in a boon to agricultural producers. These producers won't be the subsistence farmers who lose their land to higher temperatures in the tropics but rather the huge conglomerates that farm efficiently in temperate zones and massive greenhouses. If global warming causes their profits to spike, they aren't likely to lobby for it to be brought under control. In other words, even if the incentives for rich and poor countries to reduce global warming are broadly aligned, there will still be people for whom they are very divergent indeed.

The bottom line is this: if citizens of rich countries fail to see that their pollution is destabilizing poor countries, whose problems then rebound all over the world, they will not change their behavior. Moreover, when these incentives do become more closely aligned, it will be a sign that the poor countries have already become so unstable as to attract the attention of every consumer and decision maker in rich countries. For hundreds of millions of people, life will already have gotten much worse. Gaps between rich and poor countries will have grown much wider, because instability will have delayed and deterred growth for the latter group.

This inequality will have dramatic effects on the world, much more so than the inequality caused by the current wave of globalization. Overall, globalization seems to have reduced inequality between countries but increased it within countries. That increase, however, has been more a result of rich people getting richer than poor people getting poorer. The inequality caused by global warming will likely work in the opposite direction: poor people will get poorer as they lose their sources of food and their land loses its value. Moreover, inequality will likely worsen not just within countries but across countries as well. The potential for resentment, hatred, and war will be much greater than at any time since the end of the Cold War— and none of that will be good for the global economy.

12

THE STRUCTURE OF POLITICAL INSTITUTIONS WILL STOP THE WORLD FROM SOLVING ITS BIGGEST PROBLEMS.

As the previous chapters have shown, climate change and the emergence of a financial black market present important risks to the growth of the entire global economy, not only to specific countries. Minimizing these and other global risks will clearly require global strategies and global cooperation. Unhappily, our current frameworks for global policymaking have given politicians a set of incentives that make such cooperation extremely difficult.

The reason has to do with the shape of the solutions. Most solutions to the big problems facing the global economy involve either a long-term investment or cross-border cooperation, and our world is currently ill-equipped to do either. To understand why, let's consider these solutions one at a time.

First, long-term investment. To help poor countries deal with global warming, rich countries will likely have to invest more heavily in the poor countries' capacities or accept more of their people as migrants. Both of these actions have high up-front costs that, presumably, will be more than repaid in the future. Yet politicians have a hard time committing themselves to this kind of policy; they will be responsible for the costs, but their successors will enjoy the benefits of the payoff.

A politician with her eyes on reelection will only choose to back a long-term investment if she can be sure that the entire electorate understands the merit of what she is doing. That is not always the case. We saw this problem in the earlier chapters' discussions of government spending on research and education, the political cost of liberalizing immigration policies, and the difficulty of turning down neocolonialist deals.

Next, cross-border cooperation. To prevent poor countries from being stripped of their professional middle classes, rich countries will have to exercise self-control in cherry-picking immigration policies. Essentially, they will have to form a cartel in which they all pledge not to overfish the river of poor countries' human resources to ensure that the waters do not become stagnant. As in any cartel, though, every member has an incentive to break away, taking advantage of the others' restraint. Again, the benefit for the incumbent leaders is instantaneous, while the cost to their countries and to the rest of the world is carried over the long term. We have seen this dynamic in the rich countries' eagerness to negotiate bilateral and regional trade deals in lieu of working through the World Trade Organization, the difficulty of reaching a global agreement to cut pollution, and the emergence of the financial black market.

Both categories of solutions are hampered by politicians' inability to make long-term commitments. We must now ask, given the challenges we face, whether our governing institutions are up to the task. Do we need to change the incentives facing our leaders, so that they might make the right choices for us and for our children? If we can orient them more toward the long term, the results for the global economy will be truly stunning.

How might we do this? It is not easy, nor are all of the options immediately palatable. The most obvious, perhaps, is to lengthen terms in office. A president who serves for four years is already campaigning for the next election after two.

Would it be better to give him eight years from the start? Not only would it change his own incentives, but it would also change how his counterparts interacted with him; knowing that he would be in office for a period that in many countries is an entire economic cycle, they might be more prepared to engage in long-term projects and eschew an outlook oriented mainly toward quick political wins. The disadvantage, of course, is that his constituents might not be able to choose new leadership as soon as they might like.

An alternative is to provide rewards for leaders who institute productive long-term policies. An example of this is the Ibrahim Prize, given by the Mo Ibrahim Foundation, which rewards recently retired leaders from Sub-Saharan Africa who have avoided corruption and helped to foster sustainable development in their countries. Winners of the prize, who are chosen within three years of leaving office, receive $5 million over ten years and then $200,000 per year for life, plus up to $2 million for worthy causes in which they involve themselves after their political careers. The prize acts as a sort of earthly reward for leaders who succeed in overcoming political pressures and taking the long view.

A third idea is to try to change political, social, and economic culture at its roots by educating the next generation of global citizens in a way that emphasizes long-term planning and cooperation in the public arena. Unfortunately, this idea suffers from a sort of chicken-and-egg problem; it is a long-term plan that requires a substantial up-front investment.

Given the breakdown of multilateral institutions like the World Trade Organization and the Kyoto Protocol, as well as the failure of rich and poor countries alike to spend and live within their means, the need for a change in thinking and attitude is obvious. To ensure a better future for the global economy as a whole, we will have to begin considering the underpinnings of our political institutions as well.

This effort will have to be cooperative; a single country

cannot go it alone. Moreover, as the global economy integrates, the need for cooperation will become increasingly acute, because the risks to growth are becoming more synchronized for countries that were once far removed from one another.

Indeed, the global economy is becoming more interconnected as its size and value expand. That interconnectedness means that, at least in one sense, the global economy is becoming less diversified. In November 2009, stock markets from London to Shanghai tumbled after Dubai World, a huge conglomerate in the United Arab Emirates, revealed that it would not be able to make the payments on its debts of $60 billion. A decade earlier, this kind of financial wrinkle in the Middle East would not have had such far-reaching consequences. It is true that investors now have more places to put their money, but at the same time fewer places are insulated from troubles elsewhere.

Synchronicity can make markets more volatile, recessions deeper, and crises more contagious. When ten thousand investors in a country own stock in a company, then ten thousand investors may react when news about that company emerges. But when ten million investors around the world own stock in a company, then there are ten million reactions, plus millions more as these investors rebalance their holdings of the other stocks in their portfolios, and this makes share prices more volatile. When investors keep almost all their money in the securities of a single country (as most Americans did as recently as the 1970s), then even if they sell their holdings in one company, their money still stays in the same market. But when investors can invest in fifty countries, they may decide to use the proceeds from a sale in one market to buy stocks in another market altogether, thus sucking liquidity out of the first market; this is why countries like Malaysia started to control flows of money across their borders after the Asian financial crisis of 1997. And finally, when a country's debts are owed mainly to its own people, then a default is mainly that country's problem.

But when a country's creditors include foreign investors, those investors may balance their losses from a default by refusing to roll over the loans of other countries, putting those countries in danger of default as well; this is what happened to some Latin American countries in the wake of the Mexican crisis in 1994.

At the same time as the forces of economic integration are tying countries' fortunes closer together, they are also driving countries further apart by increasing inequality. This is a landmark change that may make cooperation much more difficult. Until recently, rapid globalization helped to reduce inequality between countries while increasing inequality within them. In the next few decades, inequality is likely to increase both within *and* between countries. Within, because people with wealth and education will continue to have the best chance of exploiting the opportunities that global economic integration can create, whether moving to new lifestyle hubs, seizing new jobs as intermediaries, or founding new businesses in their home countries or abroad. Between, because forces like the new colonialism, global warming, and trade segmentation will further tip the balances of power and expand the economic gaps between rich and poor countries.

Those gaps pose a threat to cooperation for several reasons. First, when people live very different lives, it becomes harder for them to understand or even be aware of one another's problems. When blizzards hit the northeastern United States in February 2010, politicians and pundits blithely declared that global warming was being overestimated. At the same time, several parts of the western United States were experiencing severe droughts. If these commentators can't be expected to look past their own driveways—let alone at more than a couple of weeks of data—how can they understand the consequences of the dire conditions caused by climate change in Africa, Asia, and South America? Second, it's hard for two very different countries to negotiate on equal terms, even with a supposedly level playing field. As we saw in the case of the World Trade Organization, the massive resources of rich countries combined with the powerful incentives for poor countries to submit to the rich countries' wishes can quickly give negotiations a coercive quality.

Overcoming these challenges will not be easy, but it will be essential for guaranteeing the growth that is possible in the coming decades. Millions of people will be able to live longer and more productive lives. Millions more will be able to escape poverty. As things stand, however, our political leadership is set to leave much of this growth on the table. They have every incentive to aim for short-term wins rather than long-term gains and to go it alone rather than build coalitions. The only way to change these incentives is to change the system. But don't look to the politicians themselves to change the system in which they have been successful. The impetus will have to come from the grass roots—the diffuse billions whose future is at stake. And that is the biggest challenge of all.

AFTERWORD

My goal in the preceding chapters has been to offer predictions that are provocative and occasionally counterintuitive but also eminently plausible and based on clear logic. Several of the predictions belie the conventional wisdom that appears day after day in the pages of morning newspapers and passes through the lips of correspondents on evening newscasts. They also have broad implications for the future.

For example, if China will enjoy only a short stint as the world's leading economy, then some of its partners in Africa, Asia, and Latin America may not benefit as much as expected from their political and economic relationships. If the European Union cannot maintain its economic integration, then it is unlikely that the euro will take over from the dollar as the world's leading currency. If the Internet will not, in fact, kill the middleman, then more college graduates will want to acquire the skills needed to be intermediaries rather than direct-to-consumer entrepreneurs. And if trade will actually become freer by abandoning the World Trade Organization, then many textbooks will have to be rewritten to reflect the victory of reality over theory—and the legions of politicians, civil servants, and lawyers who have tried for nine years to reach some sort of global deal should probably start to look for other work.

The analyses that led to these predictions have two fundamental pillars. Their frame of reference is an understanding of the deep factors behind long-term economic trends, and their method is to examine the dynamics of economic systems, seeing how the parts fit together and not just looking at the numbers that come out at the end. It's important to note that this method does not extrapolate. It takes nothing for granted, since what has happened in the past several years and even what is happening now may not be anything like what happens in the future. Rather, the method tries to identify the most enduring underlying processes and chains of causality, and then it asks, "If X happens, what happens next?"

At the very least, I hope these predictions have caused the reader to reconsider his or her preconceptions about how the global economy will develop in the coming decades. But the exercise of prediction is useful for another reason: it helps us to perceive new opportunities and to gauge emerging risks.

THIS book began with a cautionary note about the science of prediction based on Heisenberg's principle of uncertainty, the difficulty of simultaneously measuring where a subatomic particle is and where it is going. I will close with an analogy to a related notion from particle physics.

In the 1930s, Erwin Schrödinger wanted to demonstrate that the kind of indeterminacy noted by Heisenberg could create bizarre situations if applied to real life. He used the example of a cat in a box that might be exposed to poison, depending on whether an atom decayed or not. Until you opened the box, you didn't know if the cat was alive or dead. As a result, the cat simultaneously existed in states of life and death that would not be realized until you opened the box.

Predicting the future of the global economy has something in common with Schrödinger's famous cat, who to this day exists both alive and dead in the pages of countless textbooks. At any one moment, there are innumerable possibilities for the state of the global economy. Yet once we begin to predict what may actually happen, we start to narrow down those possible states. It is only necessary for one person to react to a prediction in order to change the future of the global economy, placing it on one path rather than countless others.

It is my hope that this book will have exactly that effect, and, in the same spirit, I hope that the exercise I have recorded here will be repeated sporadically in the future, whatever that future may bring.

NOTES

The following sources supply publicly available statistics used in this book:

Economic growth, United States:
Bureau of Economic Analysis, www.bea.gov

Economic statistics, Association of Southeast Asian Nations:
www.aseansec.org

Employment statistics, United States:
Bureau of Labor Statistics, www.bls.gov

Government budgets, Brazil:
Brazilian Institute of Geography and Statistics, www.ibge.gov.br

Industrial production, United States:
Federal Reserve Board of Governors, www.federalreserve.gov

Internal trade statistics, European Union:
Eurostat, ec.europa.eu/eurostat

Output and trade statistics, various countries:
Central Intelligence Agency World Factbook, www.cia.gov/library/

publications/the-world-factbook; International Monetary Fund, www
.imf.org

Population estimates and projections, United States and selected
other countries:
U.S. Census Bureau, www.census.gov

Population estimates, China:
National Population and Family Planning Commission of China,
www.npfpc.gov.cn

Trade agreements, history, disputes, and statistics, worldwide:
World Trade Organization, www.wto.org

1: China will get richer, and then it will get poorer again.

11   *In China's 2000 census* National Bureau of Statistics, People's
      Republic of China, *Fifth National Population Census* (final values,
      2002), via the United Nations Statistical Division online data-
      base of demographic statistics, www.data.un.org.

11   *A 2003 report by Goldman Sachs* Dominic Wilson and Roopa
      Purushothaman, "Dreaming with BRICs: The Path to 2050,"
      Global Economics Papers, no. 99 (October 1, 2003).

12   *Martin Jacques, the author of a book* Paraphrased from comments
      made by Jacques on *BBC World News*, June 25, 2009.

15   *Early calculations showed that* N. Gregory Mankiw, David Romer,
      and David N. Weil, "A Contribution to the Empirics of Eco-
      nomic Growth," *Quarterly Journal of Economics* 107/2 (May 1992).

15   *conditional on their ability to export* Shin-ichi Fukuda and Hideki
      Toya, "Conditional Convergence in East Asian Countries: The
      Role of Exports in Economic Growth," in *Growth Theories in
      Light of the East Asian Experience*, ed. Takatoshi Ito and Anne O.
      Krueger (Chicago: University of Chicago Press, 1995), 247–65.

15   *Conditional on having similar economic* N. R. Vasudeva Murthy
      and Victor Ukpolo, "A Test of the Conditional Convergence
      Hypothesis: Econometric Evidence from African Countries,"
      Economics Letters 65/2 (November 1999).

15   *China had steadily lost ground to its industrializing neighbors*
      Michael Pettis, using statistics compiled by Angus Maddison,

"China's Relative Economic Growth During the Past 80 Year [*sic*]," *RGE Monitor*, June 10, 2008.

16   *As his regime continued* Gordon G. Chang, "China After 30 Years of Reform, I," *Forbes*, December 16, 2008.

16   *Two factors that economists regard as particularly important* Philippe Aghion and Peter Howitt, *The Economics of Growth* (Cambridge: MIT, 2009).

18   *Confucianism is perhaps the leading influence on Chinese business practices* Ministry of Culture, People's Republic of China, "The Confucian Ethics and the Traditional Chinese Business Culture," www.Chinaculture.org (2003).

18   *the* People's Daily, *China's influential state newspaper* Ming-Jer Chen, *Inside Chinese Business: A Guide for Managers Worldwide* (Cambridge: Harvard Business School, 2001).

18   *Though Confucius himself did not view* Daniel A. Bell, *China's New Confucianism: Politics and Everyday Life in a Changing Society* (Princeton: Princeton University Press, 2008).

19   *As the management researchers Yuan Fang and Chris Hall point out* Yuan Fang and Chris Hall, "Chinese Managers and Motivation for Change: The Challenges and a Framework," Proceedings of the 15th Annual Conference of the Association for Chinese Economics Studies, Melbourne, Australia, October 2–3, 2003.

19   *Maximizing profits is not necessarily the government's only goal* Donald C. Clarke, "Corporate Governance in China: An Overview," *China Economic Review* 14 (2003): 494–507.

19   *Research shows that government-dominated companies* William Bradford, Chao Chen, and Song Zhu, "Ownership Structure, Control Chains, and Cash Dividend Policy: Evidence from China," Center for China Finance and Business Research Working Paper Series, no. 20 (2007).

19   *Publicly traded Chinese companies can have as many as five classes of shares* Daqing Qi, Woody Wu, and Hua Zhang, *Pacific Basin Finance Journal* 8/5 (October 2000): 587–610.

20   *which tend to concentrate the instruments of power* Sonja Opper and Sylvia Schwaag-Serger, "Institutional Analysis of Legal Change: The Case of Corporate Governance in China," *Journal of Law and Policy* 26 (2008): 245–69.

20   *the government has been known to use the legal system* See, for example, the case of Stern Hu, an executive of Rio Tinto who

was arrested, held without charge, then held beyond the end of an investigation after negotiations about the price of iron ore between the mining company and the government broke off.

20   *a recent video series presented by* The Atlantic It was written by Bob Schapiro and produced by Dovar Chen, *On the Frontlines: Doing Business in China* (2009).

21   *business negotiations in China tend to be based* James K. Sebenius and Cheng (Jason) Qian, "Cultural Notes on Chinese Negotiating Behavior," Harvard Business School Working Paper Series, no. 09-076 (December 24, 2008).

22   *One study completed in 1999 suggested that younger managers* David A. Ralston et al., "Doing Business in the 21st Century with the New Generation of Chinese Manager: A Study of Generational Shifts in Work Values in China," *Journal of International Business Studies* 30 (1999).

25   *Japan had an urban-to-rural population ratio like China's ratio today* Ministry of Internal Affairs and Communications, *Historical Statistics of Japan*, www.stat.go.jp (2009), chap. 2.

26   *A report published in 2007 by the International Labor Organization* International Labor Organization, "Visions for Asia's Decent Work Decade: Sustainable Growth and Jobs to 2015," August 13, 2007.

26   *According to estimates by the United Nations* United Nations, "World Population Prospects: The 2006 Revisions (Highlights)" (New York: 2007).

2: The European Union will disintegrate as an economic entity.

34   *Italy was struggling with a deep recession* Sandrine Boyadjian, "Impact of the Crisis on the Italian Economic Cycle," *Crédit Agricole EcoNews*, no. 135 (October 7, 2009).

34   *The failure to accommodate led several experts and pundits* See, for example, David Frum, "Euro Breakdown?" *National Post*, December 13, 2008; or Martin S. Feldstein, "Will Euro Survive the Current Turmoil?" *Korea Herald*, November 26, 2008.

34   *Some scholars insisted that the benefits* See, for example, Barry Eichengreen, "The Euro: Love It or Leave It?" *VOX*, at www

.voxEU.org (November 19, 2007); or Charles Wyplosz, "The Blessing of Having the Euro and the Need to Make It Better," Real Instituto Elcano Working Paper Series, no. 41 (July 21, 2009).

36 *They offered low-interest loans of up to $105 billion* Stephen Castle and Jack Ewing, "Europe Unifies to Assist Greece with Line of Aid," *New York Times*, April 11, 2010.

36 *jobs in both manufacturing and services were moving* See, for example, John Tagliabue, "Car Production Surges in Eastern Europe," *New York Times*, November 25, 2006, or Tagliabue, "Eastern Europe Becomes a Center for Outsourcing," *New York Times*, April 19, 2007.

37 *At the 13th International Anti-Corruption Conference* The author was in attendance at this session, titled "Special Session 1: Lessons Learned from the EU Anticorruption Policy," and held on November 1, 2008.

40 *The Scandinavian civil law system* Thorsten Beck and Ross Levine, "Legal Institutions and Financial Development," in *Handbook of New Institutional Economics*, ed. Claude Ménard and Mary M. Shirley (New York: Springer, 2005).

41 *Migration flows from East to West* Béla Galgóczi, Janine Leschke, and Andrew Watt, "Intra-EU Labour Migration—Flows and Policy Responses," in *EU Labour Migration since Enlargement: Trends, Impacts and Policies* (Farnham, Surrey, U.K.: Ashgate, 2009).

42 *Right now, the West subsidizes* Petr Mach, "Money-Go-Round," www.money-go-round.eu.

45 *A cautionary example of this problem comes from* This paragraph draws on a paper presented by Michael Bordo, "Does the Euro Have a Future?," Cato Institute 21st Annual Monetary Conference: The Future of the Euro, Washington, D.C., November 2003.

3: The new colonialism will leave the colonizers and the colonized worse off in the long term.

51 *Often, the Soviet Union was happy to help them pursue it* Marshall I. Goldman, "A Balance Sheet of Soviet Foreign Aid," *Foreign Affairs*, January 1965.

52 *But since 1995, when the World Trade Organization* World Trade

Organization, press release, "Transparency Deal Emerging for Developing Nations' Treatment in Food Safety and Related Issues," October 28, 2009.

53 *In Nigeria, for example, $300 billion* Paul Wolfowitz, "Transparency in Extractive Industries," speech delivered at Extractive Industries Transparency Initiative Conference, Oslo, Norway, October 16, 2006.

54 *For example, developing a natural gas field might cost $10 billion* Oliver Klaus, "ADNOC, ConocoPhillips Issue Tenders for $10B Shah Gas Devt," Dow Jones Newswires, May 25, 2009.

54–55 *Western companies haven't been the only bidders* See, for example, Reuters, "Iraq Invites Brazil Petrobras to Build Oil Refinery," April 8, 2009; or Barry Fitzgerald, "Sinopec Comes Calling," *Sydney Morning Herald*, July 14, 2008.

55 *a Chinese mining firm paid $27 billion* Panafrican News Agency, "Chinese Firm Buys Half of Nam Copper Mine," September 15, 2009.

55 *Responding to offers of land from Angola* Ron Derby, "South African Farmers Offered Land in Angola, Uganda," Bloomberg News, October 9, 2009.

55 *When Saudi Arabia's government was looking* Andrew Martin, "Mideast Facing Choice Between Crops and Water," *New York Times*, July 21, 2008.

55 *A consortium of German companies* Kate Connolly, "German Blue Chip Firms Throw Weight Behind North African Solar Project," *The Guardian*, June 16, 2009.

57 *In 2006, a government minister in Zambia* Robyn Dixon, "Africans Lash Out at Chinese Employers," *Los Angeles Times*, October 6, 2006.

57 *More recently, a report covering ten countries* Erin Conway-Smith, "Report: Chinese Bad Employers in Africa," *GlobalPost*, July 29, 2009.

57 *experts are warning that the colonizers' plans* Daniel D. Bradlow, "Large Land Deals, Outsourcing, and Responsible Development," www.voxEU.org (July 24, 2009).

57 *China's Chinalco offered to pay* John Simpson, "Peru's 'Copper Mountain' in Chinese Hands," BBC News, June 17, 2008.

58 *many of them are illiterate* Cambodia National Institute of

Statistics, *Cambodia Socio-Economics Survey 2007* (August 2009). Author's interviews for an unpublished article on Cambodian economic development provided additional material.

58 *For example, Cambodia has become one of the targets* Yee-ho Song and Sun-yoon Hwang, "Korea Seeks Cheap Land Overseas to Grow Food," *JoongAng Daily*, November 16, 2009.

58 *A program led by the World Bank issued* Statement from the World Bank on the Royal Government of Cambodia's termination of the Land Management and Administration Project, September 6, 2009.

58 *At the end of 2008* ChinaStakes.com, "China Expands Investment in South Africa and the Whole Continent" (September 7, 2009).

58 *One of those investments was a Chinese bank's purchase* Joe McDonald, "China's Biggest Bank Buys into South Africa's Biggest Lender in US$4.75 Billion Deal," Associated Press, March 4, 2008.

58 *And in 2009, China overtook the United States* Reuters, "China Becomes S. Africa's Top Export Destination," October 2, 2009.

59 *Speaking anonymously to the South African newspaper* Kgomotso Mathe, "Government Refuses to Bend in Uproar Over Dalai Lama," *Business Day*, March 23, 2009.

59 *China is losing about 8,000 square kilometers* Zhouying Jin and Ying Bai, "Meeting the Resource Challenges in China," presentation to the World Resource Forum, Davos, September 15–16, 2009.

61 *Just weeks after the government of Guinea* Krista Larson and Anita Powell, "Analysts Question $7B China-Guinea Mining Deal," Associated Press, October 14, 2009.

62 *Despite these concerns, some experts* Sarah McGregor, "Chinese Fund May Pledge $1 Billion in African Investment in '08," Bloomberg News, April 28, 2008.

62 *This tradition emphasized the rights of the individual* Open University, "The Differences between Common Law and Civil Law Systems," *Judges and the Law*, 2009, at openlearn.open.ac.uk.

62 *In the postcolonial period* Andrei Shleifer, "The New Comparative Economics," *NBER Reporter* (Fall 2002).

62 *The Chinese legal system* Jerome A. Cohen, "The Plight of

Criminal Defense Lawyers," statement presented at U.S. Congressional-Executive Commission on China Round-table Discussion on Challenges for Criminal Justice in China, Washington, D.C., July 26, 2002.

62–63   *The legal systems of the Gulf nations* Ahmed al-Suwaidi, "Developments of the Legal Systems of the Gulf Arab States," in *Finance of International Trade in the Gulf* (London: Graham & Trotman, 1994).

63   *and does not recognize the concept of a corporation* Timur Kuran, "The Absence of the Corporation in Islamic Law: Origins and Persistence," *American Journal of Comparative Law* 53 (July 2005).

63   *At its core is the idea* Robert Barro, "Democracy and Growth," *Journal of Economic Growth* 1/1 (March 1996).

65   *Under pressure from citizens* BBC News, "World Bank Tackles Food Emergency," April 14, 2008.

65   *predictably eliciting protests from import-dependent countries* P. K. Abdul Ghafour, "Kingdom to Put Pressure on India to Ease Rice Exports," *Arab News*, April 20, 2008.

68   *A three-year program will attempt to build* Wagdy Sawahel, "China-Africa: Three-Year Partnership Plan Announced," *University World News*, November 29, 2009.

4: Changing immigration policies in rich countries will worsen the brain drain from poor countries, even as they get richer.

72   *is frequently an economic necessity* Daniel Altman, "Shattering Stereotypes About Immigrant Workers," *New York Times*, June 3, 2007.

72   *In the past one hundred and fifty years in the United States* This and subsequent statistics are from U.S. Department of Homeland Security, *2008 Yearbook of Immigration Statistics* (August 2009).

73   *tens and perhaps hundreds of thousands of refugees* BBC News, "Refugees Flee from Darfur to Chad," February 10, 2008, news.bbc.co.uk.

73   *The number of illegal immigrants* Michael Hoefer, Nancy Rytina, and Christopher Campbell, "Estimates of the Un-

authorized Immigrant Population Residing in the United States: January 2006," *Population Estimates* (August 2007).

77   *In line with mainstream economists' best thinking* See, for example, Dan Vergano, "Science Funding May Rise Under Obama," *USA Today*, April 27, 2009.

77–78 *It is well known that the Social Security System* See, for example, the summaries of the Social Security Administration's annual reports, at www.ssa.gov/OACT/TRSUM/index.html.

78   *in 2005 the nation was spending only 6 percent* Anna D'Addio and Edward Whitehouse, *Pensions at a Glance* (Paris, France: Organization for Economic Cooperation and Development, 2009).

79   *South Korea's government science foundation* Daniel Altman, "U.S. Paradise Lost?" *International Herald Tribune*, October 20, 2005.

81   *you have to live there for twelve years* BBC News, "Swiss Reject New Citizenship Rule," June 1, 2008.

81   *may fall by as much as a quarter by 2050* Ryuichi Kaneko et al., "Population Projections for Japan: 2006–2055; Outline of Results, Methods, and Assumptions," *Japanese Journal of Population* 6/1 (March 2008).

81   *Foreign-born people constitute only 1.6 percent* Junichi Ihara, speech delivered at the reception for the Japan-America Student Conference, Los Angeles, August 7, 2008.

81   *a United Nations envoy found* Doudou Diène, "Racism, Racial Discrimination, Xenophobia and All Forms of Discrimination: Addendum, Mission to Japan," United Nations Commission on Human Rights, January 24, 2006.

81   *the productivity of workers in the United States* Dale W. Jorgenson and Koji Nomura, "Economic Growth and Information Technology in the U.S. and Japan," presentation at the Economic and Social Research Institute, Cabinet Office, Tokyo, June 25, 2007.

82   *only 60 percent of the working-age population* "Labor Force Survey: Monthly Results," Statistics Bureau, Japan Ministry of Internal Affairs and Communications, September 2009.

84   *A report released by the Arab League* Emirates News Agency, "100,000 Arab Scientists, Doctors and Engineers Emigrate Annually," September 5, 2009.

84   *Another study suggested that vast numbers* Fitzhugh Mullan, "The Metrics of the Physician Brain Drain," *New England Journal of Medicine* 353/17 (October 27, 2005).

84   *the government of New Zealand* Daniel Altman, "New Zealanders, 'Please Come Home,'" *International Herald Tribune*, February 15, 2006.

85   *emigration rates for college-educated people* Andrew Burns and Sanket Mohaptra, "International Migration and Technological Progress," *Migration and Development Brief*, no. 4 (February 1, 2008).

5: The backlash against capitalism won't last, but it won't be replaced by political stability, either.

92   *placing Bolivia among the ten most unequal countries in the world* As per the Gini coefficient, which rose to 60.6 in 2002.

95   *a survey of 141 large companies* Watson Wyatt Worldwide, "Effect of the Economic Crisis on HR Programs," Update: April 2009.

95   *companies are reluctant to sue employees* I owe this point to H. Michael Boyd, interviewed by Lorraine Lawson for an article published on www.TechRepublic.com, June 28, 2000.

96   *even as income differences between countries have narrowed* See, for example, International Monetary Fund, "Globalization and Inequality," in *World Economic Outlook 2007* (October 2007); or United Nations, "Trends and Patterns of Inequality," in *Report on the World Social Situation 2005: The Inequality Predicament* (August 2005).

98   *The planned surges of industrialization* See, for example, William Easterly and Stanley Fischer, "The Soviet Economic Decline," *World Bank Economic Review* 9 (1995): 341–71; and Dwight H. Perkins, "Growth and the Changing Structure of China's Economy," in *China's Modern Economy in Historical Perspective* (Stanford: Stanford University Press, 1975).

100   *the government has steadily divested from the country's major industries* Ivar Ekman, "Sweden Prepares a Wave of Privatization," *International Herald Tribune*, March 5, 2007.

103   *In early 2009, with oil prices hovering around $40* BBC News, "Chávez Cuts Budget Over Oil Price," March 22, 2009.

6: Americans will become the world's sales force.

114   *Since the early 1970s, the distribution of college majors* Author's calculations based on National Center for Education Statistics, *Digest of Education Statistics* (Washington, D.C.: U.S. Department of Education, September 2008).

114   *and the share of American high school graduates* Ibid.

115   *the Bureau of Labor Statistics has forecast* U.S. Bureau of Labor Statistics, "Overview of the 2008–18 Projections," in *Occupational Outlook Handbook, 2010–11 Edition*, at www.bls.gov/oco/.

118   *An advertisement placed in* Harper's Weekly It is available at advertising.harpweek.com; originally published in *Harper's Weekly*, March 23, 1872.

118   *One advertisement in* Harper's Weekly *for Vin Mariani* Addiction Research Unit, University of Buffalo Department of Psychology, "Before Prohibition: Images from the Pre-Prohibition Era When Many Psychotropic Substances Were Legally Available in America and Europe," www.wings.buffalo.edu/aru/preprohibition.htm (September 20, 2001).

123   *the spread of English as a second language* David Graddol, *The Future of English?* (London: British Council, 2000).

123   *Until 2009, its entire architecture* Agence France-Presse, "Internet Inches Closer to 'Internationalisation,'" November 16, 2009.

124   *The fast-food chain McDonald's, for instance* Robert Winder, "Of Course, They Can't Really Curry Flavour," *The Independent*, June 20, 1999.

125   *Take the example of Masi Oka* Min Lee, " 'Heroes' star Masi Oka says 'Lost' helps pave way for shows with Asian characters," Associated Press, August 29, 2007; Hal Boedeker, "Pressure Is On for 'Heroes,'" *Orlando Sentinel*, August 9, 2007; and web video from Fuji Television.

7: As the global economy integrates, the middleman will win.

131   *The Alibaba website calls itself* This and other information is from the company's website, www.news.alibaba.com/specials/aboutalibaba/aligroup/index.html.

132   *cross-border purchases grew more than tenfold* United Nations

Conference on Trade and Development, *World Investment Report*, September 2008.

132 *its worldwide revenues topped $2 billion* From www.bakernet .com/BakerNet/Firm+Profile/Our+History/recentyears.htm.

133 *some of the latest work in economic theory* Pranab Bardhan, Dilip Mookherjee, and Masatoshi Tsumagari, "Middlemen Margins and Globalization," mimeo, Boston University, June 26, 2009.

134 *Even in its own backyard* See, for example, Georgia East, "Nigerian Film DVDs Fly Off the Shelves in South Florida," *South Florida Sun-Sentinel*, September 17, 2007; and Michael Sasso, "Pirates of Bollywood," *Tampa Tribune*, September 25, 2005.

135 *Consider two of the biggest producers and processors of ideas* Full disclosure: I worked for the *New York Times* from 2001 to 2003 and its subsidiary, the *International Herald Tribune*, from 2004 to 2008. We parted on cordial terms. Potential conflicts aside, I don't think anything I write here can be as damning to the company as the precipitous drop in its share price, as detailed in this chapter.

137 *in 2008 the* Times *had about five million* Janet Robinson, "The New York Times Company," presentation at the Bear Stearns 21st Annual Media Conference, Palm Beach, Florida, March 11, 2008.

137 *as many as 80 million more potential readers* Howell Raines, "My Times," *The Atlantic*, May 2004.

137 *CNN's profits rose sharply from 2004 onward* Neil Midgeley, "Tony Maddox: CNN Squares Up to Sky and BBC in 24-hour News Battle," www.Telegraph.co.uk, June 24, 2009.

138 *until The New Yorker profiled Lee in 2003* Tad Friend, "Remake Man," *The New Yorker*, June 2, 2003.

138 *In countries like Argentina* Based on conversation with Patricia Ofaro, who worked as a Lacoste local designer in Buenos Aires.

8: The collapse of the World Trade Organization will unlock new gains from trade.

144 *notably the legions of Korean farmers* See, for example, Sylvia Hui, "South Korean Farmers, Celebrities Kick Off Protests at Hong Kong WTO Meeting," Associated Press, December 13, 2005.

144   *In fact, the ministerial meeting in Geneva* From the WTO's website, www.wto.org/english/thewto_e/minist_e/min09_e/min09_e.htm (accessed February 24, 2010): "In his report to the General Council on 17 November 2009, Pascal Lamy said that while the upcoming WTO Ministerial Conference would not be a negotiating session, it would be 'a platform for ministers to review the functioning of this house.'"

145   *for example, in 2007 the WTO found that the U.S. Commerce Department's* World Trade Organization, *WTO Dispute Settlement: One-Page Case Summaries* (2009).

146   *The World Bank estimated in 2006* Kym Anderson, Will Martin, and Dominique van der Mensbrugghe, "Doha Policies: Where Are the Payoffs?" in *Trade, Doha, and Development: A Window into the Issues*, ed. Richard Newfarmer (Washington, D.C.: World Bank, 2006).

147   *was discussing the possibility of introducing a common currency* Karen Percy, "Asian Leaders Ponder Common Currency," ABC News (Australia), October 26, 2009.

148   *Mercosur, the South American trading area* Notimex News Agency, "Arias y 'Lula' mencionan posibilidad de acuerdo Mercosur-Sica," June 4, 2009.

148   *With time, these blocs will consolidate themselves* A student, Elisa Seixas de Souza, brought to my attention that Bradly J. Condon also hinted at the consolidation of blocs in his book *NAFTA, WTO, and Global Business Strategy* (Westport, Conn.: Praeger Publishers, 2002), though his vision of it was somewhat narrower.

9: A new set of lifestyle hubs will replace today's business hubs.

160   *Leeson was able to cover his tracks* Alan Waring and A. Ian Glendon, "The Collapse of Barings Bank," in *Managing Risk: Critical Issues for Survival and Success into the 21st Century* (Andover, U.K.: Thomson Learning, 1998).

164   *A rough measure of the attractiveness of a country to mobile professionals* The formula I used here to rate each country is (Gross Domestic Product in purchasing power parity/Gross Domestic Product in dollars) x (Human Development Index

squared) x (Global Peace Index). The Human Development Index is squared, because differences in the index between countries with low scores probably aren't very important to mobile professionals; in other words, they might perceive a wider gap between Germany and Libya (index values of 0.947 versus 0.847) than between Liberia and Niger (0.442 versus 0.340), even though each pair is separated by almost the same amount on the index's scale. Countries with scores higher than 5 on the Global Human Rights Index were rejected; a score of 6 corresponds to "extensive political imprisonment," "unlimited detention," and common "political murders and brutality." Countries with scores lower than 4 on the International Property Rights Index were also rejected. The countries scoring exactly 4 were Algeria, Ecuador, Pakistan, and Zambia. Several small countries were not included because of missing data. The GDP and Human Development Index scores are for 2007; the other indexes were published in 2008 and 2009.

166 *For instance, investors in Bahrain* Arcapita, "Bahrain Bay Officially Launched with Unveiling of Masterplan & Support of Major Global Developers," press release, December 12, 2006.

166 *The city, called Bahrain Bay, will be 60 percent residential* Daniel Altman, "Bahrain Builds a City in the Most International of Ways," *International Herald Tribune*, October 16, 2007.

168 *it is ranked by the World Bank as the easiest country* Penelope J. Brook et al., *Doing Business 2010* (Washington, D.C.: World Bank, 2009).

168 *foreign companies doing deals in both of those countries* Daniel Altman, "With Interest: Waiting for India," *International Herald Tribune*, December 23, 2005.

168 *India has lifted a ban* Christopher Guly, "Indian Market Opening Up," *The Lawyers Weekly*, April 3, 2009.

168 *And foreign firms looking for a foothold* Nick Parsons, "Considerations When Selecting Regional Headquarters," www.Asialaw.com (June 2007).

169 *going through the Northwest Passage* Dominique Kopp, "Russia: The Polar Grab," *Le Monde Diplomatique*, September 2007.

169 *Even in a country where freedom of speech is limited* Reuters, "Jobless Migrant Workers Protest in Singapore Again," February 27, 2009.

169   *with an average high temperature* Wee Kim Wong et al.,
        Yearbook of Singapore Statistics, 2009 (Singapore: Depart-
        ment of Statistics, 2009).

169   *Singapore's population is aging steadily* From the U.S. Cen-
        sus International Data Base, www.census.gov/ipc/www/
        idb/.

171   *In 2009, for example, the government of Dubai* Neeraj Gan-
        gal, "Dubai Plans Start-up Help for Expat Entrepreneurs,"
        ArabianBusiness.com (November 20, 2009).

10: An enormous financial black market will arise outside of traditional centers.

This chapter includes material from interviews with Andrew Lo and Markus Brunnermeier, and with Robert Glass and Walter Beyeler of Sandia National Laboratories. Some of the material was previously published in Daniel Altman, "The Network," *The New Republic*, October 22, 2009.

180   *the little fund from Connecticut* ERisk Case Studies,
        "LTCM—Long-Term Capital Management," www
        .erisk.com.

181   *In Washington, the heads of the major financial regulators*
        From author's interview with a former official of the
        Clinton administration who was present during these
        events but insisted on anonymity.

182   *Many big banks were holding assets and liabilities* Daniel
        Gros and Stefano Micossi, "The Beginning of the End
        Game," www.voxEU.org (September 20, 2008).

182–183 *Researchers and officials from the bank sat in different rooms*
        From author's interview with an official of the European
        Central Bank who participated in the simulation but
        insisted on anonymity.

183   *investors and financial institutions were using this market
        to cover* Bank for International Settlements, Statistical
        Annex, *Quarterly Review* (June 2008).

187–188 *De Larosière came back with an eighty-six-page report* Jacques
        de Larosière et al., *Report of the High-Level Group on Finan-
        cial Supervision in the European Union* (Brussels: European
        Union, February 25, 2009).

189   *In his public comments, the meeting's host* BBC News, "Brown Urges End of 'Tax Havens,'" March 14, 2009.

190   *Financial firms couldn't make millions using derivatives*
      For Enron, see Daniel Altman, "Enron Had More Than One Way to Disguise Rapid Rise in Debt," *New York Times*, February 17, 2002; for Greece, see Louise Story et al., "Wall St. Helped to Mask Debt Fueling Europe's Crisis," *New York Times*, February 13, 2010.

191   *Just consider what Derek Adler* Alicia Green, "BVI Embraces New Era for Offshore Centres," *Hedgeweek* (November 2009).

192   *A report on the British Virgin Islands published in 2004* International Monetary Fund, "British Virgin Islands—Overseas Territory of the United Kingdom: Assessment of the Supervision and Regulation of the Financial Sector, Volume I—Review of Financial Sector Regulation and Supervision," *IMF Country Reports*, no. 04/92 (February 28, 2004).

192   *A similar report on the nearby Turks and Caicos Islands* International Monetary Fund, "Turks and Caicos Islands: Assessment of the Supervision and Regulation of the Financial Sector—Review of Financial Sector Regulation and Supervision," *IMF Country Reports*, no. 05/24 (August 31, 2004).

193   *the Cayman Islands is home to about 10,000 hedge funds* Caribbean Net News, "Cayman Islands Monetary Authority Marks 10,000th Fund Registration," December 2, 2005.

195   *the way the United Kingdom bailed out its citizens* BBC News, "Icelandic Bank Savers Bailed Out," October 8, 2008.

11: Global warming will make rich countries cleaner and richer and poor countries dirtier and poorer.

200   *More than a decade ago, the economist Jeffrey Sachs* See, for example, Andrew D. Mellinger, Jeffrey D. Sachs, and John L. Gallup, "Climate, Coastal Proximity, and Development," in *Oxford Handbook of Economic Geography*, ed. Gordon L. Clark et al. (New York: Oxford University Press, 2000).

201   *Baseline predictions of global warming* Susan Solomon et al., eds., "Climate Change 2007: The Physical Science Basis," *Contribution of Working Group I to the Fourth Assessment Report of the Intergovernmental Panel on Climate Change* (New York:

Cambridge University Press, 2007); compiled by NASA Earth Observatory as "Future Temperature Changes," www.epa.gov.

201   *The Intergovernmental Panel on Climate Change* Michel Boko et al., "Africa," in *Contribution of Working Group II to the Fourth Assessment Report of the Intergovernmental Panel on Climate Change*, ed. M. L. Parry et al. (New York: Cambridge University Press, 2007); with population projection from the U.S. Census International Data Base.

201   *In Latin America, the panel found* Graciela Magrin et al., "Latin America," in ibid.

201   *And in Asia, as many as 132 million people* Rex Victor Cruz et al., "Asia," in ibid.

203   *They are immensely polluting* See, for example, Jessie Boylan, "Charcoal a Dirty Trade-Off," Inter Press Service, November 19, 2009.

205   *In a memo that was leaked* "Let Them Eat Pollution," *The Economist*, February 8, 1992.

205   *when companies from rich countries break laws* See, for example, Elisabeth Rosenthal, "Smuggling Europe's Waste to Poorer Countries," *New York Times*, September 26, 2009.

205   *when the local governments are too corrupt* See, for example, Beata Smarzynska Javorcik and Shang-Jin Wei, "Pollution Havens and Foreign Direct Investment: Dirty Secret or Popular Myth?" in Don Fullerton, *The Economics of Pollution Havens* (Cheltenham, U.K.: Edward Elgar Publishing, 2006).

206   *There are plenty of questions* See, for example, Cahal Milmo, "The Big Question: Does Carbon Offsetting Really Help in the Fight Against Climate Change?" *The Independent* (January 11, 2007).

207   *especially if they end up selling cheaply* Reuters, "EU Carbon Price Could Crash Again: Report," August 9, 2007.

209   *Deforestation, which has been blamed* United Nations Integrated Regional Information Networks, "Deforestation Exacerbates Droughts, Floods," November 10, 2006.

210   *In some regions of India* William R. Cline, *Global Warming and Agriculture: Impact Estimates by Country* (Washington, D.C.: Center for Global Development and Peterson Institute for International Economics, 2007).

210   *indeed, this is already occurring* Lisa Friedman, "Cities Swell with Climate Migrants," ScientificAmerican.com (March 16, 2009).

211   *as Sachs has called them* Jeffrey D. Sachs, "Climate Change Refugees," *Scientific American*, June 2007.

212   *Half of the money, according to Brown* BBC News, "UK and France Propose Climate Fund for Poor," November 28, 2009.

213   *Overall, globalization seems to have reduced* See, for example, Paul Collier and David Dollar, "The Economic Effects of the New Wave of Globalization," in *Globalization, Growth, and Poverty* (Washington, D.C.: World Bank, 2002).

12: The structure of political institutions will stop the world from solving its biggest problems.

218   *Dubai World, a huge conglomerate in the United Arab Emirates* Associated Press, "A Look at Dubai World Holdings," November 27, 2009.

218   *(as most Americans did as recently as the 1970s)* Martin S. Feldstein and Charles Y. Horioka, "Domestic Saving and International Capital Flows," *Economic Journal* 90/358 (June 1980).

219   *in February 2010, politicians and pundits blithely declared* See, for example, Shaun Tandon, "US Climate Skeptics Seize on Blizzard," Agence France-Presse, February 11, 2010.

219   *several parts of the western United States were experiencing* Brian Fuchs, "U.S. Drought Monitor," Lincoln, N.C.: National Draught Mitigation Center, available at drought.unl.edu/dm/monitor .html, February 11, 2010.

ACKNOWLEDGMENTS

As in my previous books, I feel that I must thank the many government agencies and international organizations that offer free access to their data and publications online. It is true that tax revenue pays for the collection of many of those data and the issuance of many of those publications, and citizens have a right to see what they're buying. Nevertheless, the easy-to-use websites maintained by these groups are a valuable asset in the service of informed citizens and democracy as a whole. I owe special thanks to the *Doing Business* team at the World Bank, who also shared their offline data on two occasions.

In the closing stages of writing this book, I was also teaching a course at New York University's Stern School of Business on the future of the global economy. Most of my ideas were fairly polished by that time, but the students in the class helped me to refine some of them and also offered valuable new points of view. For that I thank them. Countless friends were also sounding boards for my ideas, perhaps unknowingly, and I am grateful for their willingness to debate in English and Spanish. (Some did not need to be prompted. You know who you are.)

Apart from those conversations, the writing of this book

was basically a solo voyage. The publication was not, however, and I heartily thank the various people who made it possible, notably Larry Weissman, Paul Golob, Dedi Felman, and Robin Dennis. I also thank Vijay Vaitheeswaran for encouraging me to air my ideas more broadly.

In my research, I may have missed the work of people with ideas similar to mine. This book does, after all, take on a big topic on which many scholars and pundits have already commented. I can only ask those people's forgiveness and assure them that any lack of attribution is due to deficient reading rather than deficient writing.

Finally, I thank my family and friends for their enduring support.

INDEX

Malaysia
  control of flow of money across
    border of, 218
  as home to lifestyle hub, 164,
    165
Malta, 30
Mao Zedong, 15
Marcos, Ferdinand, 51
mass media, 120–21
McDonald's, 124
media. *See* mass media
Mercosur, 148
Messi, Lionel, 122
micro-capitalism, poor countries
    and, 83
Middle East
  emigration from, 84
  migrant workers in, 76
middlemen
  economic globalization and,
    130–34
  in the future, 139–41
  intellectual property and,
    134–38
  lifestyle hubs and, 162
  role in industries dealing with
    tangible goods, 138
  role in selling into foreign
    markets, 139
Mo Ibrahim Foundation, 217
Moldova, 93
Monsoon Wedding, 134
Montevideo, 161
Mookherjee, Dilip, 133
Morales, Evo, 66, 92
Murray, Bill, 125
Myanmar, 64

Nair, Mira, 134
Namibia, 55

National Science Foundation, 79
natural resources, 71
Nespresso, 125
Netherlands
  changes in government of,
    45
  European Coal and Steel
    Community and, 30
  long-term economic potential
    and risk for, 40, 41
network maps, 186–87, 196
New York Times, The, 135–36,
    137
New Zealand
  attempts to lure back
    expatriate population, 84
  immigration points system of,
    80
Nicaragua
  political movement in, 92
  purchasing power of, 104
Nigeria, 53, 64, 65, 122
Niyazov, Saparmurat, 102
Noble Drilling, 113
Nollywood, 122
North Africa, 84
North Korea
  isolation of, 98, 102
  socialism and, 102
  U.S. assistance to, 91
Norway, 60

Obama, Barack
  global cap-and-trade system
    and, 203
  global reaction to election of,
    121
  green business and, 112
  National Science Foundation
    and, 79

ABOUT THE AUTHOR

DANIEL ALTMAN is the author of *Connected: 24 Hours in the Global Economy, Power in Numbers* (with Philippe Douste-Blazy), and *Neoconomy*. He is the director of thought leadership at Dalberg Global Development Advisors and the founder and president of North Yard Economics, a not-for-profit consulting firm serving developing countries. He previously wrote economics columns for *The Economist,* the *International Herald Tribune,* and *The New York Times,* and currently teaches at New York University's Stern School of Business. He lives in New York City.